*Simran,*

# LETTERS
## TO A YOUNG
# LIFE
## COACH

*For We Are All Young in This Field*

*Thank you for all of your help.*
*May your biggest dreams come true.*

*Faith*

FAITH J. POWERS

For inquiries, please contact Faith J. Powers at her business website:
www.thinkwellcoachingandconsulting.com

E-book ISBN: 978-1-7320826-0-1
Print ISBN: 978-1-7320826-1-8

For all Young Life Coaches,
no matter your stage,
you are wanted.

# THE LETTERS

Dear Young Life Coach,

Somehow this book has found its way to you. It might be a gift from a loved one. It might be a loan from a friend. It might be a suggestion from a colleague. It might be a recommendation from a well-visited website. Whatever its path, this book has found its way to you.

Now, the question is what are you to do with it? The answer, of course, is up to you.

What follows are a series of letters meant to speak to you, no matter your stage in the *Life Coaching process*. For advanced coaches, this may be the book you wish had been written when you were first starting out, one you are picking up to serve as a touchstone to the first few steps of your Life Coaching career, or one you are perusing as you think about the legacy you will be leaving. For those recently started on the *journey* to becoming a *Life Coach*, this might be your ally, your friend, the volume you can turn to when you *want* to just be with Life Coaching. For those who hadn't considered, until now, that they might want to become a Life Coach, this may be your introduction to the field, the collection of words and paragraphs that change your life forever.

No matter who you are or where you are in the process of coaching, this book is meant for you. Its aim is to be a safe place for you to think about coaching and to feel about coaching. To determine what coaching might do for you and what you might do for coaching.

I welcome you, Young Life Coach. For we are all young in this field. That is one of coaching's many gifts: the *beginner's mind*, which, in my experience, also fosters a beginner's heart and spirit.

Sincerely,
Faith
A Fellow Young Life Coach

Dear Young Life Coach,

You might be wondering why I am calling you by that title. After all, you haven't truly considered becoming a Life Coach. Likely, this book was a gift from someone or something you picked up on a whim because it sounded interesting. It's no matter.

What is important is this: You are here, giving yourself the *opportunity* to learn about something new, even if that learning experience lasts for only a few letters or sentences. You will find, if you keep reading, when it comes to Life Coaching, credit is given where credit is due – both to the smallest steps forward and the biggest leaps of faith taken. Also, exploration is treasured.

So, treasure yourself for making it this far, Young Life Coach, if you are willing. And, if you'd like, you can explore your *thoughts*, by asking yourself these questions. What do you think of when you picture treasuring your *efforts*? What comes to mind? What *feeling* does that bring up? Is it something you want to experience more of?

Life Coaching *clients* often do.

This *appreciation* of *self*, this craving to get to know self is often what draws seekers to the process of Life Coaching. Whether they be seekers of meaning, seekers of adventure, seekers of dreams. Self and this desire to get to know self creates the first appointment as it once did the field.

And in this piece of knowledge lies the crux of Life Coaching: Life Coaching is as much a part of life as life is a part of Life Coaching. The two are inseparable. Which is how I knew, how I know, even if you finish with this letter, you, too, are a Young Life Coach.

The field is pleased to meet you, Young Life Coach, as am I. I look forward to seeing what else you choose to do with your self and your life.

Sincerely,
Faith

Dear Young Life Coach,

Your journey to becoming a Life Coach began with an idea. This idea might have tapped at your attention while you were exercising. It might have surfaced while you were transporting your children to or from school. It might have come to you as you were transitioning from one *life phase* to another. It is fitting your Life Coach dream began with an idea. Ideas are what Life Coaching is all about.

Now that you have that idea—the Life Coaching idea—the question becomes what do you do with it? Again, the answer lies in you.

So, how do you find that answer? How do you discover what you want? This is where the magic of Life Coaching begins.

There are many questions you can ask yourself. Some of those questions deal with *whats*. Others with *hows*. *Whens*, *wheres*, and *whos* will come up, too. And Life Coaching, masterful Life Coaching, will always lead you to the *whys*.

So, perhaps, we can start there. Why?

Why has your mind suggested you might want to Life Coach? Is the why an experience? Something connected to a positive moment in your *past*? Something saying you can have more of this, more of me, if you only try? Is the why a coming together of you, the many different sides of you, in the *present*? Sides you haven't fully tapped into, or even known existed, until now? Or is the why a *vision*, the beckoning of your *future* and all of its possibilities? The landscape of potential that pulls you from bed in the morning?

You know. Even if you don't know you know, you do.

This is one of Life Coaching's greatest lessons. One that is learned over and over again. The answer always lies in you.

No matter where the idea of Life Coaching came from and no matter where you want to go with Life Coaching, you will be checking in with yourself, sitting with yourself as you likely haven't in a long *time*, and *listening*. Listening to the beauty of your own thoughts. Marveling at the way they are strung together. Understanding, deeply understanding, how much the mind can do.

By listening to yourself, you are engaged in what artists and explorers have been engaged in for ages. Discovering the previously undiscovered. Creating the previously uncreated. Pursuing the previously unpursued.

If you are in your first *act of life*, this may be the job you have dreamed of for some time. You may have actively looked at schools, craving an education, wanting to be grounded in the science of coaching, as well as the art.

If this is your second act of life, you may be adding this work to another career or this work to a family, enriching your experience, balancing out your pursuits.

If this is your third act of life, you may have accomplished what you wished to accomplish in your earlier years. You may be eager to reinvent yourself—to try something new or to reconnect with the seed of a dream you first thought about planting years ago.

No matter what act you are in, no matter your reasons for being here, you are thinking about Life Coaching. You are sorting through the fragments, statements, and paragraphs your mind produces. You might even be collecting information, feeding this process, trying to decide if Life Coaching is right for you.

This is good, Young Life Coach. This is where you are and should be at this stage. You are thinking about Life Coaching. And Life Coaching, more than any other field, appreciates your thoughts.

Sincerely,
Faith

Dear Young Life Coach,

Your mind may be filled with thoughts now, some about Life Coaching, some about other things. Allowing yourself to think will do that. Thoughts, when given a space to exist, tend to come alive.

When yours are on Life Coaching, you might realize you don't know how to define the term exactly. Sure, your mind might be able to produce a general concept, generate a basic picture. But, you wonder, does it have the right concept? Does it have the right picture?

In truth, there is no right concept, no right picture, not as an absolute.

There are guideposts, though, markers that can help you understand the field and your place in it. Some of those guideposts are the answers to a standard set of questions you may be asking yourself. What is Life Coaching? What is it not? What is a Life Coach supposed to do? What not?

Let's start with these. It is a good place to start.

Do you want to be a supporter of thinking? Do you want to be a pioneer of dreaming? Do you want to be a connector of wants and whys to the who—the Client? If so, you want to be a Life Coach.

On the other hand, are you looking for the opportunity to tell someone what you know about what to do? Do you have more knowledge about processes and correct *approaches* than you can keep inside? Are you waiting for someone to ask you, "How? How do I do this?" so you can say, "Here. Here, I'll show you." If so, you want to be a consultant.

Are you ready to delve into someone's past? To figure out how a person ticks? To explore *strengths* and target *weaknesses*? To provide *tools* for replacing unhealthy *patterns* with healthy ones? To deeply explore a person's *conscious* and *unconscious* mind in order to help that person move beyond *suffering*? If so, you want to be a therapist.

No matter what you want to do, there is an avenue for achieving it. And each avenue has value.

If *consulting* is what calls to you, you can add it to your *skill* set and offerings. You just won't be doing so as a Life Coach. If *therapy* is what speaks to you, you can pursue a degree and help others heal themselves. Again, this pursuit will be outside of the realm of Life Coaching.

If Life Coaching is what draws you, though, beautiful, wonderful Life Coaching, then you are ready to begin. You are ready to learn the process, to grow to trust the process, so you can help others become who they always wanted to be.

Take your time, Young Life Coach. Enjoy the journey. There is so very much to learn.

Sincerely,
Faith

Dear Young Life Coach,

At this stage, you may be wondering, "Who does Life Coaching serve?" The answer: Anyone with a *dream*. Anyone who is willing to pursue a better life. Anyone who wants to move beyond *surviving* to *thriving*.

How? Sometimes, this is where the how comes in. Such a question is typical at this stage. And this is a good place to address it.

Life Coaches work with others, *collaborate* with others, to help them think, to help them define what they want to keep and what they want to change, as they move from this day to the next. The arena of Life Coaching is the future.

Though all action must be taken in the present, the horizon is where the Life Coach's vision is trained. Together, coach and client look toward where the sun rises, over the terrain across which the client will step. The treasured there is a guidepost. The journey the true center of conversation.

And there is appreciation. So much appreciation.

Every Life Coaching conversation includes some form of appreciation—from the respect shown by asking the client, "What would you like to do some thinking about," to the validation of listening to the specific *feedback* that travels from coach to client and client to coach. Appreciation is truly at Life Coaching's *core*. This is often one of the most enticing aspects of the experience for both members of the *Thinking Space*.

Challenging can happen, too. A *challenge* that is honest and presented gently can be one of a Life Coach's greatest tools. Often, challenges come when the client has a thought that is blocking a path that would otherwise be traversed, the heavy intellectual boulder that just won't budge. Interestingly, it isn't muscle or magic that moves the *block*. It is an idea, a thought that brings into question the existence of the boulder itself. The block is self-created and it is self-removed through the beauty of understanding and reframing.

If the block truly exists, if it is based in fact, the size of the intruder is often what changes. The once scary stone is reduced to a mere pebble or set of pebbles that can be stepped over or removed, piece by piece.

If the block is less substantial, if it is mere shadow, then its true *identity* is unearthed. Client and coach watch as it fades, disappears, allowing the client to continue on down a now unfettered path.

If it is somewhere in between, real pieces are separated from what is unreal. And each is dealt with accordingly.

Life Coaching makes such feats possible.

And, in the process, Life Coaching transforms people—both coach and client, in their individual ways. Each *session* of Life Coaching centers on the client's wants and wishes. Each session also helps the coach to see more clearly, to listen more swiftly, to understand more adeptly. In short, Life Coaching is the meeting of two minds that belong to two human beings who become more themselves with every passing conversation.

So, now you have a little information about the who of Life Coaching. And the how.

What more you can imagine about the who? And the how? What other questions rise from the depths of your mind?

We will speak again soon, Young Life Coach. Until, then, embrace your questions. Be sure to hold your thoughts close. They are your new treasured territory. And what a beautiful territory indeed.

Sincerely,
Faith

Dear Young Life Coach,

It's at this stage that you might be wondering about the branches of Life Coaching, the limbs attached to the grand tree. In truth, there are as many branches as there are human beings.

The coaching experience is different for everybody. No two clients see coaching the same way. No two individuals experience coaching the same way. No two clients want the same thing. This means there are more and more ways to do Life Coaching, more and more focuses in Life Coaching being developed every day. You, too, may invent your own *specialty* one day.

Life Coaching in the business world is often called Executive Coaching. It may also be called Business Coaching, Career Coaching, Corporate Coaching, or Professional Coaching. It has many facets. Some are to match workers to positions, some are to prepare leaders for promotion, some are to enhance workplace harmony.

Life Coaching in the private sphere is often known by its original name. Or just Coaching. You may also see qualifiers and specifiers attached, to help interested parties find their perfect fit.

For those looking to improve their *relationships*, there is Relationship Coaching, Family Coaching, Parent Coaching, Couples Coaching. The word Life may be included as well.

For those interested in improving their health, there is Health Coaching, Wellness Coaching, sometimes even Health and Wellness Coaching. The two preceding words are often listed near, if not next to each other.

For those interested in general self-improvement, there is Development Coaching, also often called Purpose-Driven Life Coaching or Transformational Life Coaching.

For those facing a *transition* from one life phase to another, Transition Coaching or Transitional Life Coaching.

As can be seen, Life Coaching can take may forms. Whatever the name, wherever the service is provided, the *goal* at its core is the same: To help clients become the best versions of themselves they can be, the best versions of themselves they want to be.

This is the heart of Life Coaching—what you will discover and enjoy if you choose to join the legion of dream-supporters and value-focused beings.

For now, I must leave you to your thoughts, Young Life Coach. Your ponderings. I look forward to meeting with you again shortly. Take care.

Sincerely,
Faith

Dear Young Life Coach,

It's good to see you again. I am glad that you have made it this far. I imagine you have many questions by now, many curious inquiries.

Questions are central to Life Coaching. A curious nature is, too.

If you are wondering how those interested in Life Coaching learn to become the coaches of their dreams, you are not alone. Many want to know more about how to develop a good foundation, how to form strong roots at this stage.

Just like with the branches of the Life Coaching tree, the roots that feed its core are plentiful. They vary in size and shape. They vary in reach and length. The strongest function in very similar ways.

Have you thought about what you might want to learn? What you think is key?

Degrees are possible in Life Coaching. Curricula are being developed at an increasingly rapid pace. Full programs and subspecialties are often tied to the humanities or business, psychology or the medical field. They start in the form of associates programs and can advance to doctoral degrees. Have you heard of any of these programs? What about them sounds appealing?

Another option is the certificate, the most common method of training. The schools that offer them span the globe. Their classes vary in focus and length. From personal *transformation* to business coaching, there is something for everyone. From online attendance to weeknight meetings, there is a way for everyone.

Some programs are the brainchild of a specific individual or set of individuals. Others follow the recommended curriculum of at least one of Life Coaching's governing bodies. What do you know about certificate programs? What about them sounds interesting?

Through careful research and thinking, you can discover what works best for you. In the meantime, it might be helpful to sit with your mind, Young Life Coach, your vision, so you can decide what questions you want answered. What do you need to know before you feel prepared to take the next step forward? The length of the program? The cost? The flexibility?

Do you wish to better understand the pros and cons of having a particular certificate or degree? Are you committed to staying within a certain geography?

Is there a particular field of Life Coaching you might wish to work in? Must you tailor your training to a specific type of client, such as a governmental agency or large business, some of which require you to be certified by one of Life Coaching's governing bodies.

Because the profession is not regulated, you can hang your shingle without training. It isn't suggested. There is far too much to learn. There is also the opportunity to create a peer base, to *connect* with a community. What kind of coaches might you wish to meet?

Perhaps there is a certain personal *value* you wish to remain in contact with, to have reflected back to you as part of training? No matter the reason behind your choice, there is an educational option for you. A way to achieve *success*.

I can't wait to hear what you choose, Young Life Coach. And why. And what you think about your choice. And how you feel now that the decision has been made. I am curious as to what you most wish to learn during this part of your journey. I am excited to be informed of any or all of your discoveries. Best wishes, Young Life Coach. Best wishes. I will write again soon.

Sincerely,
Faith

Dear Young Life Coach,

You may be wondering, "How many choices must I make on this Life Coaching journey?" In truth, there are many, just as with life. Often, after deciding on a school, after gearing up for that transformational journey, a coach-in-training ponders just how far is far enough when it comes to credentialing.

The answer to that question is as individual as you are. You will decide based on what you want to do, who you want to serve, and how much you want to experience and learn.

Of course, as is true with all decisions, it can be helpful to know just a little bit about the governing bodies. As a whole, these organizations have sought to define and shape the field of Life Coaching. They have made themselves responsible for creating guidelines for Life Coaching, including ethical standards, or *ethics*, which along with *laws and rules*, help form the basis from which the foundation for best practices are developed.

That's a lot to take in I know. And we haven't even gotten to the letter combinations. Often, those will make even the most seasoned Life Coach's head spin.

One of the primary governing bodies is called the International Coach Federation, the ICF. I know. The letter combinations have already begun. Please bear with me. I will try to make it as simple as possible.

The ICF provides accreditations to programs as well as individual credentialing for Life Coaches. It's the individual credentialing that is of *purpose* here. The ICF has three levels of individual credentialing. And each of them comes with a very similar acronym. If you are a practitioner of deep breathing, take one now or two. I am happy to wait. We can carry on when you are ready. Great.

The Associate Certified Coach, otherwise known as the ACC, is the most basic level of credentialing provided. The specific guidelines can be found on the ICF's website. I will share with you the generalities. The core components are training received, hours of coaching work, and completion of an *assessment*. This is the foundation for the other two certifications as well.

There are several paths for documenting training hours, depending on the type of program attended or the substitution of a more individualized path of education. In addition, proof of mentoring by a Life Coach, called Mentor Coaching, and audio recordings of coaching sessions may also be required, depending on how and where training was received. Someone pursuing the ACC might be interested in showing individual clients that they have demonstrated their coaching abilities to those who know what coaching is and should be.

A lot already, right? I know. The letters and *requirements* can be a bit overwhelming. Just know that those daunting little bits of alphabet are manageable over time. And they often come in threes.

When you feel prepared, we can proceed to the next set.

The Professional Certified Coach, the PCC, also requires documented training, proof of coaching hours, and a passing grade on an assessment, the same assessment as required in the lower certification. The hours of coaching required are significantly more here. Proof of Mentor Coaching and audio recordings may also be required for the same reasons mentioned before. The PCC level of credentialing is what is most often required by governmental agencies and large businesses, such as corporations, when they want proof of competency. Some have been known to accept the previous standard. Still others may require nothing at all.

Okay. Now, we are on to the final set of letters for ICF's individual credentialing. The Master Certified Coach, the MCC, is slightly different in that there is only one path for achieving it. Coach training hours, Mentor Coaching, a hefty number of documented hours of coaching, submission of coaching sessions for performance evaluation, and a passing grade on the previously mentioned assessments are the requirements. There are no ifs, ands, or buts here. Individuals who pursue the MCC are likely interested in being distinguished as the top in their field and/or providing training to other up-and-coming coaches.

That's it for ICF individual credentialing. And their many Cs. It is my hope that focusing on the basic structure of the requirements has been helpful and grounding.

Now, if you are willing, let's look at the International Association of Coaching, the IAC, and its certification process. As with the previous organization that shall not be referred to by its letters here, lest such letters send anyone down the rabbit hole of confusion, the IAC has three levels of certification.

The first is called the Masteries Practitioner. There is no abbreviation listed next to these words. For some, that may be a relief. To earn a designation as a Masteries Practitioner, the IAC requires that a Life Coach pass an online test as well as submit a Masteries Professional Development Plan, which must be approved. Let's break down the words, shall we?

Masteries refers to the fact that the person submitting the plan is committed to and willing to demonstrate the IAC's proposed ingredients for good coaching. They call these ingredients and guidelines the Masteries. Professional means that the person creating this proposal intends to work in the coaching field. Development means that the individual submitting the plan is committing to continued growth and learning. Plan means the ideas being submitted are not just a form of wishful thinking, but a well thought out set of goals that allow for and can be used to track personal *accountability*; in other words, it is an *action plan*. Not that different from what coaches require of their clients in terms of commitment to a vision, right?

The IAC indicates that this particular designation can be renewed yearly though the organization states it is not required to move up the credentialing ladder. The group reports that this particular certification was created to show that new coaches are serious about their work and professional development, even in the early stages. That they are working toward *mastery*.

Let's take a *pause* now. Maybe another deep breath? Breathe in. Breath out. Good.

The IAC's next offered certification is the Certified Masteries Coach. I must warn you: The letters are back. This certification is abbreviated CMC.

The Certified Masteries Coach designation is earned through passing the test mentioned earlier as well as submitting recordings and being graded. I will refer you to the website for specific details as they can always change. That lengthily titled professional development proposal, the Masteries Professional Development Plan, is also required. Individuals who are interested in this designation are likely seeking to demonstrate their competence in terms of what the IAC considers to be good coaching.

The third and final IAC designation is the Master Masteries Coach, also called the MMC. I recognize that the name is a bit of a tongue twister. Still, the designation has its benefits.

The basic requirements for the MMC are very similar to the previous credentialing designation. The difference is that the performance on the audio recording must be rated higher for a coach to be considered masterful. Coaches interested in this designation likely want to achieve high personal competence as well as have proof of that competence available for others to see.

So, there you have it. The above are the most well known of the credentialing options in Life Coaching at this time. There are other designations available from different organizations and schools as well. Still, there are only so many letters and titles that can be suggested at a time.

Thus, I will leave you with these, Young Life Coach. Congratulations for making it through what is one of the most confusing portions of deciding on an educational path in Life Coaching. Feel free to engage in a few minutes of *self-care*. You have earned it.

Sincerely,
Faith

Dear Young Life Coach,

Now is the tricky part. At least, for many, it can feel like the tricky part. Up to this point, you have thought about becoming a Life Coach. You have learned the basics about training, credentialing, and possible career paths. You have been afforded the opportunity to sit with your thoughts and feelings.

Now, it is time for you to decide. Will you embark on this journey? Or will you bypass this path for now?

"Decisions, decisions" is a common saying. And for good reason. Decisions can have a significant effect upon thoughts and the mind. Some days, when the mind is facing a decision, it will want to go over and over and the available options. Other days, it will question the truth of what is known, often by engaging in *metathinking*, which occurs when the mind closely examines or thinks about its own thoughts and thinking process. Still others, it will wish to pause, pause for a long time before proceeding.

Now might be a good time for such a pause. Where is your mind with this decision? What seems important to review? Where is your heart with this decision? What seems important to allow yourself to feel? Have you progressed to *metafeeling*? Do you have certain feelings about your feelings?

You may, after the pause, find you are exactly where you need to be to make this decision. You may have, in your conscious *awareness*, all of the information necessary to check the yes or no box following the question, "Will I become a Life Coach?" If so, the remainder of this letter may not be necessary for you.

If not, if the information you have is swirling in your brain or if your thoughts are pulling you in two different directions, do not fear. A decision can still be made, a choice can still be had.

One thing to remind yourself is: You have made a decision before. That may sound simple, but it is an important fact. You have traversed this landscape and come out the other side.

That is a relief, right? That you are equipped for this phase? Being equipped can be a nice surprise, especially when it comes to moments like this.

If you are ready, if you would like to examine what qualifies you to handle this moment, let's take a look. Let's try a tool.

In your head is likely a list of pros and cons. Even if you have not officially gathered them together and assigned them to columns, they exist within.

On the pros side will be the things that are drawing you toward Life Coaching. The many reasons you are telling yourself to say yes. They may include a combination of what you have learned is possible alongside what you dream can come true.

On the cons side will be the things that point you toward no. They are likely comprised of the hesitations you have and may include limits on your time or *resources*.

If you would like, now might be a good time to make these pros and cons official, to jot down what you think makes the Life Coaching journey an asset as well as what you believe makes it a liability. What you think will get in the way of its successful completion as well as what resources you know you possess that can contribute to is healthy development.

The process of transcribing such pieces of information can be illuminating.

New items might be generated. Certain positives might shrink in size as you acknowledge their existence. Certain negatives might go up in smoke as you look at them more closely. What seems insurmountable might be redefined as manageable. And what seems elementary might reveal an extra facet or two.

Once you have finished, Young Life Coach, once you have sorted out what is in front of you, allow your mind to choose. Give it time. Listen to it. Respect its reasoning. Then, check in with your heart. Your heart remains a part of this choice, too. It will provide you with a feeling. That feeling has worth and deserves to be considered.

Together, your mind and heart will create *wisdom*. And it is from this wisdom that you have the best chance of choosing what it is you want to do. What will further your life in the way that is most important to you.

All that is left then is the big reveal. The one you are making to yourself. I will allow you some privacy. You deserve that.

When you are ready, when you are willing, you may let me know what you have chosen. Until then, I will be waiting. Patiently.

Sincerely,
Faith

Dear Young Life Coach,

Here we are. You have made your decision and you are ready to let me know.

You have explored all you needed to explore at this stage.

Are you on your way to becoming a Life Coach? Are you headed down this path of action?

Or are you being called to another place?

From deep inside, your answer came. Which means, no matter what you have chosen, you are well and you are on your way.

If this is it, Young Life Coach, if this is our parting, know that I bid you a wonderful adieu. Wherever your life leads you next, wherever you go, don't forget you will always house a little bit of Life Coach inside. Good luck with your journey. And know that I *support* you.

If this is not it, however, if this is just the beginning, then settle in. We have more to discuss, Young Life Coach, more to go over, more for you to learn about one of the most important people in your life— you.

I thank you for the opportunity to have accompanied you thus far. I am eager to be of any assistance I can. This process is amazing, isn't it? I can only imagine what's around the corner, what the rest will portend.

Sincerely,
Faith

Dear Young Life Coach,

Congratulations! You are here. You have decided to become a Life Coach. I wonder what, from everything you have learned, is in your head right now. What beautiful work is going on in your mind?

What beautiful work is going on in your heart?

What led you to your choice? Such a step is a determination. It also requires determination. Commitment. These are great traits, great qualities, Young Life Coach. I am proud of you. Are you proud of yourself?

How long did the decision take? Did you contemplate what you might do for a day? A week? A month? A year? A decade?

What tipped you over the scale from thinking about being a Life Coach to recognizing you are one, you have to be one?

That step, the one over the line that separates those on the outside of Life Coaching looking in from those on the inside drawing from within is a big one. It may be the same size as many a step taken before, but it is not the same.

What is unique about your step? What makes it yours and yours alone? What would you call it? A move finally taken? A necessary change? A leap of faith?

How might you recognize it? How might you *celebrate* it? What you want to do is up to you, Young Life Coach. This is your moment. This is your day.

Tomorrow, we will proceed forward. For now, all I can say is: I am so glad you are here.

Sincerely,
Faith

Dear Young Life Coach,

With each new addition to your life, with each new added *role*, a shifting will take place. This is the way of things. You will experience *role conflict*. You will be challenged to move things around in order to accommodate what is just starting.

What do you anticipate you might have to *balance*? What will fall in the plane of equal weight? What will you have to check in with to make sure that both Life Coaching and it are being appropriately tended to?

How might you achieve this?

How will you know what you can pause? What might you wish to leave for another day? What do you anticipate might have to take a backseat during this journey?

What is your plan for re-approach, for reincorporating this back into your life after such a sacrifice?

Is there anything you will have to say goodbye to, Young Life Coach? Or anything you have already said goodbye to? How do you handle goodbyes?

It is true that many beginnings have related ends. Are ends hard for you? Are they trying? Do you recognize them as something that can be called for from deep inside?

It is okay to say goodbye, Young Life Coach. And it is often necessary.

It is also okay to struggle with goodbye. Moving forward takes time.

Hellos might also be waiting, hellos other than Life Coaching. Hellos can bring with them many thoughts and many feelings. Do you have any other hellos in your life right now? Has Life Coaching's warm greeting paralleled one from another area of your life?

Or, as can also be common, has Life Coaching created for you a new opportunity? *Inspired* you to do something you've always wanted to do?

How might your hellos work together? What synergy might they create?

It is my wish, Young Life Coach, that you greet what you are happy to see with openness and intrigue. That you say goodbye to what you must say goodbye to with understanding and an appreciation for its past value. And that you remain committed to that which has been and will stay.

Whatever you brought with you, Young Life Coach, whatever pushes you forward, whatever draws you near, know that you are not alone. You and your journey are welcomed with open arms.

Congratulations, Young Life Coach. Congratulations again. You have earned it. You. Have earned it.


Sincerely,
Faith

Dear Young Life Coach,

Now that you have decided to join the field, now that you recognize your life will shift in either significant or subtle ways, you will find there are other decisions to be made.

Let's look at one of the first: Education. Have you settled upon your chosen path? Have you made it official? You have thought about it before. Has your mind changed in any way since your initial leaning?

Will you be pursuing a certificate? Or a degree? How will you be building your proper foundation? And how can you approach this next step in a way that can benefit you best?

It might be helpful to know how you approach learning, to look a little more closely at your *learning history* and what it has taught you about learning itself. Are lectures what grab your attention? Is listening a gift you bring to this phase? Are notes the way you process what you hear and see? Do you like to feel ideas enter your mind and exit through your fingertips? Are you a fan of visuals? Is a graph or a model just the thing to solidify what is being shared? Or do you prefer to jump into a task, feet first? To learn by trial? And by fire?

What do you think will work best for you here?

Beyond the basics of learning is the *schedule*. How is yours set up? Are you going to be a nighttime student? A weekend learner? Or will you be jumping all in?

What does this mean about the time in your life? Will time be a challenge? Will you have to focus more closely on *time management*? And the *timing* of next steps and activities in your life?

What about money? Do you have any concerns about how you will fund your full journey?

And other resources? Such as *energy*?

Do you anticipate you will be able to sail smoothly through? Or do you imagine a point where you might have to ask more of yourself than you imagined? How might you handle that? How have you drawn upon your strength in the past? Your reserve? Your resolve?

There are so many questions, Young Life Coach. And so many answers for which you must look within. I suppose the magic formula is to anticipate what can be anticipated and to bend when you need to bend.

I look forward to seeing how this educational process goes for you, Young Life Coach. I look forward to all the blessings it will bring. I will check in soon to see how what you imagined matches your chosen path's discoveries.

Sincerely,
Faith

Dear Young Life Coach,

I imagine your mind is swirling. Those thinking channels we opened at the beginning of our correspondence have likely been cracked further still.

It's hard to catch so many thoughts, right? To catalog them so they may be useful both today and tomorrow?

The readings you have done, what have they taught you? What stands out as helpful? How are you keeping track of what you might want to one day use?

The practice you have engaged in, what has that felt like? How have you situated yourself in that experience? What has collaboration been like for you? Being curious? Using your beginner's mind? Were they as you anticipated they might be?

What feedback have you received so far? The kind that makes you smile? The kind that makes you scratch your head? The kind that sends you off to further study?

You might not think your educators understand the change you are going through. But they do. Still, they are there to ask the best of and from you. That might be energizing if you are looking for a push. Or nerve-wracking if you haven't quite found your footing. Frustrating if you have served up what you thought to be your best. Or sad if you are having difficulty closing the *gap* between what you imagine and what you can produce.

Confusion often comes into play as well. Because there are so many concepts and so many theories. Yes, there are commonalities among those who practice. But differences, too. And how are you to know what to release and what to keep?

Your educators must challenge you, Young Life Coach. That is their job. And mine is to let you know it is okay. To balk, to quake, to grit your teeth, to go to bed early so you might rise to fight another time on another day.

As has been said, Young Life Coach, you are wrapped up in a process. You are a traveler on a journey. Each new section, each new session, has so much to show you.

The tools you have learned and those you are learning are part of your foundation and your kit. The lectures you are hearing, mentally recording, represent the words you will draw upon when questions surface. This is how the transmission of knowledge is. It provides you with just enough to have a clue, but not so much that you don't have to search for what your *solution* is.

Ask questions, Young Life Coach. Now is a time for questions. It always has been and always will be. You are not passive in this process. You have a choice in it all. That is the other message for which I am the conduit.

You are your own educational experience, Young Life Coach. You and you alone. This is a taste of life, a taste of what it feels like to be a client. And, for a budding practitioner, that is a tremendous gift.

I will write again soon, Young Life Coach. I will write to see how graduation goes. That, too, is a wondrous transition. For now, however, I will leave you to it.

Sincerely,
Faith

Dear Young Life Coach,

You are graduating from training, exiting the absorption phase of things. What's on your mind? How do you feel?

Are you still anxiously exploring the realms of meta-? *Metacommunication*? *Metabehavior*? Metafeeling? Metathinking? Do you enjoy discussing with others your ideas on the process of conversing? Have you found, as so many do, now that you understand *behavior* a bit better, you are acting differently in response to your usual patterns? Are feelings still coming in response to your feelings? And thoughts in response to your thoughts?

Or are you more aware of *metaphors*? It's strange how often we as people describe things in terms of something else, isn't it?

Wherever you are, wherever your mind is, wherever your heart rests, this time is about you. And there is much to decide. Much to do. You have completed your education or are about to. You are now ready to choose how you will use what you have learned.

What more do you know about what Life Coaches do? Are there specific niches that are of interest? Specific populations that suit you best?

What type of environment would you like to work in? Is the highrise of a corporation calling? Or the four walls of a small business?

Do you want to focus on one type of service? Or would you like to swipe your thinking brush all over life's pallet?

What would you most like to do for your clients? Most like to be? How can you bring that dream to fruition?

Would a *visualization* help now? Perhaps a perfect day exercise? One focused on Life Coaching? Can you imagine what your ideal coaching day would like look like from the *beginning* through the *middle* to the *end*? A day that is free of things you have to *tolerate*? One that is filled with sessions that inspire and fulfill you?

Or is a *relaxation technique* better suited to allow you to clear your mind and release stress from your body so you can proceed?

Transitioning from learning to *doing* is a special time, a time when vision meets action, when *belief* creates proof.

During this stage, questions emerge, often in torrents. Some are those that have already been asked and which you thought you had answered. Others are novel, brand new.

Some are welcomed. They seem to be leading you to the place you wish to go. Others you'd rather not be acquainted with. They dig deep or ask too much, at least for now.

Some remind you of a time that preceded Life Coaching. Perhaps challenge you to incorporate this new side of yourself with the successful shades of you that have come before.

Others show you what might exist. In yourself and others as a result of this Life Coaching stream.

When these questions come, they can crowd your head and make it difficult to think. It's not surprising. During a transition, you are often straddling two mindsets. So, for a time, your perspective is double. You have tasks left to accomplish as well as ones to imagine, to create. You have a mental map for how you can do both with only one mind to do the thinking.

Such conflict, such competition for your resources can create a desire to act, just so it will all be over. Though this energy is commendable, Young Life Coach, the solution is often to be present. Just to be present. It is from such presence that clarity comes, that direction comes, that you are able to sew together your own guiding tapestry.

To aid with this process, Young Life Coach, to help you sit with the in-between, you might wish to take a deep breath, to *reframe* this portion of the process so that any segment that is deemed unwanted can be understood as necessary.

Deep breaths, Young Life Coach. Deep breaths. They have a way of erasing immediacy. There is no point in rushing this. Rushing won't do now.

When you are ready, only when you are ready, you can further define your goals. Until then, honor how far you have come. Be proud of what your aspirations are. Explore how you wish to incorporate your values into it all.

This is your life, Young Life Coach. Your life. I look forward to seeing you make it all it can be.

Sincerely,
Faith

Dear Young Life Coach,

Goals. Goals are the next stage of this process. Sorting through the myriad of ideas, selecting from among them, defining successful completion, attaching timelines. Goals are their own sort of starting off point. They solidify both what is most wanted and what is needed.

What goals are you wanting to set, Young Life Coach? What plans do you have in mind? What big things must you do?

What small steps do you think will lead you there? How do you plan to engage? To ensure you have proper follow through?

How many life areas are calling for you to set goals? Creating concrete plans in one can catalyze solid direction in another. Are your goals strictly related to Life Coaching? Or has this endeavor inspired an entirely new transition?

How do you work with your goals, Young Life Coach? Do you write them down in a list? Do you record them on a calendar? In what way do you measure your *progress*? Do you tick off the different steps?

Are you a fan of the S.M.A.R.T goal method? Do Specific, Measurable, Attainable, Realistic, and Timely mean something special to you? If so, how do they apply here?

Do you prefer to brainstorm? To empty your head of all of your great ideas? Then cross things out, whittle them down until what is most important stands out?

What do you do next? Do you select one-month, three-month, six-month, and twelve-month time frames for which to create objectives? How specific do you get with your goals? Do you have some broken down into tasks in a day? Are others best suited for working on across a week? What do you do if you have a slip in your accountability?

I am curious, Young Life Coach. How do you work with goals? And which ones are most important for your Life Coaching journey?

Would it help to sit with one for a second? To bring that idea up in your head? To allow your mind to flesh it out until you see a flash of the possible *result* of that goal's completion?

Is what you see a picture? Is it a reel of a perfect day? What are the details? Where are you? What is happening? What age are you in your imaginings? Might your life appear transformed across the span of only a few years? Or are you decades older, decades wiser, providing yourself with counsel so you might know what you most want? What you most value?

Goals are magnificent, Young Life Coach. They are the application of dreams to reality. They mean you don't just wish for something, you are determined to secure it, to create it. Goals are as much a part of the beginning of Life Coaching as they are the end. They bring clients to your door. They are what your clients take with them each time a call finishes.

Goals are to be respected, Young Life Coach. And you may find they show you respect as well. When they are well-devised, when they are nourished, when they are made to matter, they can help you create the life you want. And isn't that why you are here? Isn't that why your clients have been and will continue to spend time with you?

Good luck with your goal setting, Young Life Coach. We will check in with goals again soon. For now, I leave you to your planning. I can't wait to see what comes of your applied creativity, your honed imagination.

Sincerely,
Faith

Dear Young Life Coach,

By now, you have set a few goals, made a few choices about your business. What has been solidified? What is clear in your mind?

Have you defined your *ideal* client? Doing so is something suggested by just about every source related to Life Coaching. What does your ideal client look like? Sound like? What does your ideal client want to work on?

Have you identified the client or clients for whom you might not be the best match? The thought that you might not aspire to work with everyone or that everyone might not benefit from your efforts is a hard concept at first. It is a necessary one though. An important one. Saying no can be just as coach-like as saying yes.

What is your plan for handling *referrals*? Will you be creating a network of professionals whom you trust? People who might want to work with clients other than those you are most interested in. Or people who work in sub-fields that fall outside of your areas of focus. Will you be touching base with these individuals on a regular basis? Will this be over the phone or in face-to-face meetings?

Have you already identified people from your training to whom you will turn for support? New members you can add to your *support network*. Are they in a similar phase as you? Or are they slightly ahead of or behind you? Will you be comparing *welcome packets* and handouts? The finer points of *confidentiality* and *disclosure*? Or are you wanting to discuss with them the deeper parts of your experience?

Have you sought Life Coaching from someone already in the field? This is suggested time and time again across Life Coaching tomes. Do you have a *mentor*? Someone who is guiding you through the process?

What about your location? Where will you be coaching from? The comfort of your own home? An RV on the go? A conference room in a corporate building? An office that you rent or own?

How many hours do you plan to work each week? What portion of those hours involves direct contact with your clients? What portion session prep? How many minutes per day must you devote to bookkeeping? Bill paying? *Session notes*? General organization and tidying?

What is your projected overhead? If you have decided on a location, you will have a good idea about this. If not, how do you plan to do further research? To determine what will work within your budget?

What are you seeking to make in your first year of Life Coaching? Your second? Your third? Have you settled upon your fees? Created a *fee schedule*? Will you require your clients to pay a *retainer*?

How big do you see your business growing? Might you want to provide office space for future Young Life Coaches one day?

The questions that can be asked, the ones you have already set before yourself and those you will one day pose to your own mind, can go on and on. Creating a Life Coaching business is a process, much like everything else we have discussed. There is no stationary endpoint named done. No finish line. Yet, for those who manage their time and their energies, there is much room for happiness and *joy*.

It is this I leave you with, Young Life Coach. The idea that Life Coaching can be a fountain of happiness and joy. It is why many have entered the field before you. And the reason many will enter in the years to come.

Do not forget happiness, Young Life Coach, amidst all else you have to do. Joy would enjoy hearing from you as well. Take care. Be sure to take care. We'll speak again soon.

Sincerely,
Faith

Dear Young Life Coach,

I hear you have started your business. Congratulations. Where are you? What are you doing? Are you happy with your choice?

Have you had the chance to settle in? To develop a *routine*? To find your *flow*?

What is as you thought it would be? What looks slightly different? What are you glad has surprised you? What do you wish to work more on?

Goals are one thing, Young Life Coach. Execution can be quite another. Sticking to what has been decided is commendable. So is adapting to the unexpected.

The ability to adapt is found in the most successful people, whether they be business owners or influential leaders. This is important not only to know but to give yourself credit for. This is how enterprises blossom.

What thoughts are calling out for your attention? How do you plan to check in with these? Will you be sitting with your progress on a daily basis? Do you prefer weekly? Or would monthly feel most comfortable to you?

Do you have professional as well as personal thinking sessions scheduled? If so, what do you plan to bring to your Life Coach? What do you want to do some thinking about? What would you like to put on the table in terms of accountability?

How far are you in this new enterprise, Young Life Coach? What milestones have you already met? Are you just past opening your figurative or literal doors? A commendable success, I must point out. Or are you several months in? Have the growing pains started yet?

Where are you in terms of *stages of change*? Are you over-whelmed? Still trying to identify and acknowledge everything you must work on and through? Or are you well past acceptance?

There are so many aspects to starting a new business. So many challenging and rewarding particularities. There are *risks* to be taken. And often the fear of *failure* to overcome.

How are you documenting these stages for yourself? Are you cap-turing them in pictures? Are you jotting them down in a journal? Or is your mind its own sort of video camera? Are you blessed with that kind of memory?

Starting a business is such a wonderful accomplishment, Young Life Coach. Such a bright step for such a bright you. I look forward to your many future successes. I will check in with you soon.

Sincerely,
Faith

Dear Young Life Coach,

How are things going? With both your business and you? You've had time now to settle. To surmise that dreams, goals, and visions are not always written in the same ink or by the same pen.

What significant compromises have you had to make, Young Life Coach? Sometimes, talking about these alterations can help you through the change. Or even after.

Did your adjustments primarily have to do with timelines? Did building a client base take longer than expected? Or did you suffer from the opposite trend? Were you offered the opportunity to serve more than you imagined? Did life *factors* drive you to accept the challenge laid at your feet?

These are common alterations, Young Life Coach. Very common. You are not alone. Know you are not alone.

Life Coaching, as a venture, acknowledges this. Is based on this in a way. Think about it. If you look back over your time in coaching, if you really concentrate, you will notice many of the clients you have seen bring with them the fruits of seeds they previously planted. This is true whether your clients are individuals or groups, whether they are seeking general assistance or something very specific.

Many of your clients, many of the people who show up at your door, want to know how to make what is now what was once seen. They want to feel empowered even amidst the adaptations. You listen to their original conceptions when you help them. You listen to what exists currently as you support. You identify the new seeds they have added. And you guide them toward the future. You guide them by helping them build and benefit from their own thoughts. That is your job. That is where you must focus your sight.

I wonder if you can do that for yourself, with your own *calling* to coach. I wonder if you can collect information from your past, your present, and the visions of what you want to come in order to craft your future. Your future. In doing so, you must not forget your successes, Young Life Coach. There is room for growth. Yes. There is always room for growth. There is also room for celebration. And replication of what you have done well.

Celebration can be the life breath of further reaching.

What do you wish to celebrate? What does the part of you that allows for such things want to shout from the mountaintops? Or have dinner over with a friend?

And how does that tie into what your mind tells you it wants? And your heart?

What do you seek, Young Life Coach? What do you seek?

And what will you do with this information, the products of this mid-process check-in? By looking over all you have done so far, by naming what it is you still wish to do, what avenues have you uncovered? What avenues are beckoning to be explored?

Do they include adding new client populations? Ones you didn't know you were passionate about helping until now? Do they include stepping away from a service you currently provide so room opens up for something you know you want to do? Or something you can't quite put your finger on but feel confident you will discover in time? Maybe exploring how to become more comfortable with *being* as a Life Coach? Now that you have a period of significant doing behind you?

Are there platforms you wish to access that you haven't before? Are you yearning to create an app where people can check-in and benefit from your ability to connect them to their own inner wisdom? Do you wish to record a thought-centered exercise that clients can use on the go? Do you want to introduce others to what you do through a video? Is it a visual welcome packet that you conceive of? Or an animated comparative *Life Wheel*? A sample coaching session? Or a summary of your top ten favorite tools?

What do you want, Young Life Coach? What do you wish to add to your life and your business? As long as you are engaged in this field, wants will be important. Wants will always be important. It's okay to regularly check in with yours. In fact, it is imperative that you regularly check in with yours. You assist others. You must also advocate for your self. That's right. Your. Self.

Take care, Young Life Coach. Want-away. Want. Away. I will write again soon.

Sincerely,
Faith

Dear Young Life Coach,

Having a Life Coaching business is not new to you. Nor is it old. It can never be old. Your business is like you—young forever.

You are evolving, constantly evolving. And, sometimes, that evolution is more challenging than it has been at others. You might be feeling on edge, like there is an energy inside you that you are having difficulty releasing, a *talent* you have yet to explore. Or you might be less enthusiastic than you once were. You might be craving a new challenge, an inspiring *invitation*. Your mind might be drifting to different opportunities, wanting to *stretch* further than it has before. Or you might be *stuck* on something, one thing that has yet to sparkle with its promised clarity.

This has happened before, Young Life Coach. This has all happened before. Not only across the years of human existence, but in your own life. The good news is: You have already evolved in your own life and successfully.

It's a tricky balance at times, having enough to stimulate your mind and *passions* so that everything does not feel like old hat. It's a tricky balance at times, setting limits so you are not running, constantly running, with no hope of catching up.

As a Life Coach, you have been talking with others, helping them to get where they wish to go, to become their best selves. Now, you might find, you want a little of that attention turned toward you. If you've already been giving yourself that attention, maybe you want more and in concentrated doses.

You will know. Because, somewhere within you, you recognize that your best self can look different at different stages. It will look different at different stages.

Perhaps a *theory* that focuses on human growth and its stages is a good thing to discuss here. Perhaps it is a helpful place to start.

You may have heard of Abraham Maslow's hierarchy of *needs*. Many Life Coaches have, though not all. At the top of the pyramid of human experience, past physiological needs, safety needs, belongingness and love needs, and esteem needs, is *self-actualization*. There are many ways to define this, either by drawing upon Maslow's words or the words of his followers.

The simplest way, the shortest way to describe the meaning of the term self-actualization is to say it is an experience of being one's best self. Notice I said an experience.

Part of the secret of understanding self-actualization is knowing it isn't a destination. These moments occur over time, closer and closer together, as you get better at knowing who you are and what is most important to you.

Where are you in terms of self-actualization? Can you think of a time when you tasted what it was like to be who you are in the best way possible? Are you craving a sip of that now? How strong is that urge? Likely pretty strong, especially at this stage.

This is standard, Young Life Coach. Wanting to be more you increases with each previously met need. It is what meeting those needs is driving you towards.

There will always be more for you to discover. More of you to bring into the world. More to do. More to think. More to feel. Always, there is more of you to reveal.

So, let's look closely, Young Life Coach. What do you see? What do you want now?

Would it help to check in once more with your vision of a perfect day? Or would making a list, editing it, and unearthing a selection of new goals feel right to you? What about saying hello to that wiser version of yourself? Could this you, this future you, help sort out any present haziness or confusion?

What match is begging to be lit? What parts of you long to burn brightly for days, weeks, months, maybe even years to come?

Maybe you will find the next phase of your journey won't take you far. Maybe you are where you need to be. Maybe you are doing what you want to do. Maybe you simply want to further reconnect with the beginning of your beginner's mind. To bathe in its purity. Maybe enrolling in a few continuing education classes is enough for now. Maybe it will put a spring in your Life Coaching step.

Maybe you want more, however, something more complex. Maybe you are at the apex of another transformation. Maybe you are about to transform your Life Coaching career completely.

Maybe you want to write a Life Coaching book? To discuss the intricacies of client *coachability* and the best ways to help the client *clarify* what is being said. To teach the upcoming generation of coaches about the importance of showing *interest* in the client and why it is best to let the client choose and finalize any *homework* to be completed between sessions. To illustrate the use of *humor* and *play* as well as the importance of being *childlike*. To explain how to teach the client the difference between control and *influence*. To present a method for discussing *core beliefs*. To explore how being deeply listened to boosts the client's *self-esteem*.

Or maybe you would like to make a training video? To show new coaches how to use *open-ended questions* instead of *close-ended questions*. To demonstrate the form and use of *powerful questions*, which provoke thinking in the client and *empower* the client to move forward. To showcase the importance of *clean language* so those new to the process can see what using a client's own words does for thinking. To, via your example, help ease the nervousness that many have about setting *boundaries*.

Or maybe you want to make sample Life Coaching sessions available for purchase? So Life Coaches teaching those new to the field have tools at their disposal. So they can show their classes examples of when a coach uses *mindfulness* or *intuition*. So they can help their students understand what to *mirror* looks and sounds like. So those being trained can see what happens when both the coach and the client are *open* to the process. So new coaches can understand the benefit of a coach asking a client's *permission* to share an anecdote or engage in a *teaching moment*. So they can watch an experienced coach move a client from *reporting* to working. So they know how to label *shoulds* when they come up in a session and how to help the client get to wants. Or even how to ask a client to provide a *testimonial*.

Maybe you are about to add a completely unrelated facet to your professional repertoire. Maybe you want to engage in a fourth, fifth, or sixth act, to extend beyond the basic three-act structure. To add to your list of *contributions*.

Maybe your change is inspired by the personal. Maybe there are relationships to explore or travels to pursue. Maybe there are hobbies to take up. Maybe you don't know yet, but you're sure you want something new.

There is no wrong way to self-actualize, Young Life Coach. No wrong way to bring positives to your life and the lives of others. You have built your foundation upon good principles. You have based your work on them. Maybe what you long for is to spend time with your fun principles.

Fun can be a blessing. You know that. You've been fighting on the side of joy for quite some time. As a professional in this field, you know fun can be a necessity. It is not always a trapping.

Wherever you wish to go, Young Life Coach, whatever you wish to do, know that I support you. I support your decision to continue to honor your self, to discover your self, to be kind and good to your self. To become your best self. It will benefit you. It will also benefit your clients and humanity. It is enough, though, that it will benefit you.

Carry on, Young Life Coach. I will leave you to chat with your new dream. This process is wonderful, isn't it? Magnificent. It is never done. What a comfort that can be.

Sincerely,
Faith

Dear Young Life Coach,

How are you doing? How are you feeling? Are you focused on maintaining the new goals you have set? Are you far down the new avenue you have created?

The road you have just traversed is called renewal. You have gone through this phase and come out the other end. What was it like? How long did it take? Were there echoes of this change in other areas of your life?

Phases of renewal can be trying, even if they often bring with them such great benefit. Phases of renewal can send your thoughts in all different directions. They can cause you to question what you have done. They can cause you to question who you are. Such inquiries often bring with them the standard assortment of feelings—confusion, frustration, happiness, sadness, worry.

This is all typical. All paths are evaluated at one point or another. In fact, all paths are evaluated at multiple junctures.

You have faced what you needed to face, Young Life Coach. You have used the information you collected to make adjustments in your business or your life.

What changes did you make? What directions did you keep? What resources did you require to get going?

Do you anticipate you will face renewal again in the future? What are your thoughts about that? Your feelings?

What are you working toward now? How are you staying faithful to what you value deeply? Do you have a shorthand method, a selection of words that guide you through the process? Do you have a quote you hang on your wall? A reminder on your phone? What allows you to keep an eye on what matters most to you?

If this is your first pass through renewal, know that it may not be your last. If this your first time maintaining such a big adjustment, know maintenance is ever-present in all the things we do.

If you have, however, renewed yourself before, how can you leverage those successes to help you now? If you have faced maintenance and its own unique challenges, what have you learned about keeping on with keeping on? What lessons are most salient to you? What lessons can you apply here?

Goals, as we have discussed before, can help. They can be essential. What else might be of assistance? What support has worked for you up until now? What self-care have you engaged in? What care have you received from others?

No matter your years in the business, Young Life Coach, there is much to see and much to learn. Life Coaching, like you, is forever youthful. Renewal helps maintain that youth. The maintenance that follows is key as well.

I leave you to do what you do best, Young Life Coach. To succeed at being you. To cycle through thoughts, to navigate feelings, to follow your future, and treasure what it brings. Congratulations, Young Life Coach. Congratulations. This time just for being.

Sincerely,
Faith

Dear Young Life Coach,

We meet at your next transition. You have spent the time you wish to spend with Life Coaching, as a formal affair at least. Now, what you desire is to look over your career, to review the highlights, to understand the legacy you will leave.

You have touched many lives. It was impossible for you not to. No one can coach without touching lives.

You have helped people to reach their dreams. Helping individuals connect with their values is now old hat to you. Helping them source their *motivation* and create good *habits* are well-worn skills, too.

You have introduced the importance of thriving into a populace of those who now live, in some ways, like you. They understand the significance of wanting as well as of *gratitude*.

You have helped other coaches to enter the field as well. Either by example alone or through formal instruction and mentoring.

Is it strange to think about how much you have learned from this process along the way? Is it weird to know that by providing a service to your clients your life was touched in return?

What stands out to you in this moment, at this time, with this wealth of success behind you? What is a favorite among your many contributions?

Is where you are where you imagined you would be? Have you surpassed some of your dreams?

I wonder how this feels for you. As you know, you will never leave behind the Life Coach inside. But, as you shut your doors, figurative or literal, like with every other phase, thoughts and feelings will stream.

Which ones do you wish to capture? Which ones do you leave to run free?

I will miss you, Life Coach. We will all miss you. The field is better because of you. The world is better because of you.

Thank you. Truly. Thank you. For living your dream.

Sincerely,
Faith

Dear Young Life Coach,

In closing, I find I want to make a *request*. This isn't too far off from what we have explored. Life Coaches make requests all of the time.

Mine is simple, if you would hear it.

I ask you to live your best life, your fullest life, no matter what shape that takes. Give yourself time. And the space to think. Don't forget feelings. Checking in with your feelings is important, too. I wish you joy, happiness, whatever word most closely resonates.

Be to yourself what you are to others. Know such an investment is critical. Be *authentic*. Be genuine. Be an embodiment of what you've learned and what you help others to see.

Be your self. Your true self. That self is awesome and a gift.

There you go. That is my request.

As for this time with you?

I would like to thank you, Young Life Coach, for inspiring these pages. For sharing with me a process that will never end. Thank you for the brand of collaboration you have helped me to create. It's been amazing.

It has been a honor to know you, Young Life Coach.. An honor to accompany you on your journey.

This is not goodbye. This will never be goodbye. Only good luck for now. Good luck. I have full confidence in you and all you are capable of being.

Sincerely,
Faith

# THE REPLIES

# NOTES ON THE REPLIES

### "While reading the letter…"

The questions found under this heading are general questions. They ask you to think of what was going on in your mind when you first encountered the letter. Also, they ask you to think about what feelings such thoughts brought with them.

These questions are the same for each letter, but the answers will differ based on the material presented.

### "While reviewing the letter…"

The questions found under this heading are specific questions. They pertain to a single letter and include actual questions asked therein or those inspired by what was mentioned.

The questions differ for each letter as will the answers.

### Please Know

This is a safe place for you to explore your thoughts and feelings, to be honest, and to get to know what you envision for yourself – your self – and your future. As such, it is requested that you engage only with the questions that speak to you, no matter the type and number. Write as little or as much as you wish. There is no right or wrong way to reply.

You may want to scribble your answers on blank paper or print them on a page that is neatly lined. You may want to type your answers on a computer or voice record them on a device, such as your phone. Please use whatever method works for you.

If you are a fan of privacy, I ask that you store your answers in a place only you have access to. The goal is for you to feel comfortable while sitting and speaking with yourself.

Also, if these questions bring up anything unexpected, or anything that you would like help dealing with, do not hesitate to reach out to a professional. A close family member or friend may also be of assistance, depending on what is uncovered.

Thank you for the opportunity to be a part of your journey, Young Life Coach. You are treasured.

## The Introduction Letter:
## On Who These Letters Are For
## and How They Might Be of Service

### While reading the letter...

What questions came up in your own mind?

What thoughts did you have?

What made you pause and ponder?

What do you want to know more about?

What do you want to look deeper into?

What feelings came up for you?

What positives did you remember or recollect about your self or past experience?

What did you appreciate about your self or your talents?

What did you envision for your future?

**While reviewing the letter...**

What stands out about the phrase Life Coach? How do you define it? What feeling does that bring up for you?

Are you able to recall a time it seemed like you were coaching someone? If so, what did that look like?

What were you thinking during that unofficial session? What were you feeling? What do those thoughts and feelings teach you now?
Are you able to picture yourself Life Coaching in the future? If so, what does that picture look like?

What are your thoughts about that future experience? What feelings come up when you think of that future experience? What do your thoughts and feelings teach you?

What do you think of when you see the term beginner's mind?

Are you able to recall a time when you had a beginner's mind? What did that look like?

What thoughts come to mind when you think of that experience? What feelings? What do those thoughts and feelings teach you?

Is there a place you would like to have a beginner's mind in the future? What does that look like?

What thoughts do you have about that vision? What feelings do you have? What do your thoughts and feelings teach you?

## The Pre-Contemplation Letter:
## On Thoughts You Had Before You Considered
## Becoming a Life Coach

### While reading the letter...

What questions came up in your own mind?

What thoughts did you have?

What made you pause and ponder?

What do you want to know more about?

What do you want to look deeper into?

What feelings came up for you?

What positives did you remember or recollect about your self or past experience?

What did you appreciate about your self or your talents?




What did you envision for your future?

**While reviewing the letter...**

What do you think of when you picture treasuring your efforts? What comes to mind?

What feeling does treasuring yourself bring up? Is that feeling something you want to experience more of?

How would you define a thought?

How would you define a feeling?

What does a Life Coaching client look like to you? Sound like to you?

What do you imagine that client wants from Life Coaching?

What does the term appreciation mean to you?

When have you received appreciation in your life? When have you given it?

What do you think of when you see the word self? What does self mean to you?

What stands out to you about your self presently?

What might you like to see as part of your self in the future?

# Contemplation Letter # 1:
## On The Life Coaching Dream
## and Your Relationship to It

### While reading the letter...

What questions came up in your own mind?

What thoughts did you have?

What made you pause and ponder?

What do you want to know more about?

What do you want to look deeper into?

What feelings came up for you?

What positives did you remember or recollect about your self or past experience?

What did you appreciate about your self or your talents?


What did you envision for your future?

## While reviewing the letter...

What idea led you to Life Coaching?

What do you plan to do with that idea?

Has your mind suggested to you why it might want to Life Coach?

Is the why related to something in your past? If so, what is it? How do you see it fitting in with your Life Coaching dream?

Is the why related to something in your present? If so, what is it? How do you see it shaping your Life Coaching dream?

Is the why related to you future? If so, what is it? How do you see it guiding your Life Coaching dream?

## Contemplation Letter # 2:
## On What Life Coaching Is, What It Isn't,
## And What That Means for You

### While reading the letter...

What questions came up in your own mind?

What thoughts did you have?

What made you pause and ponder?

What do you want to know more about?

What do you want to look deeper into?

What feelings came up for you?

What positives did you remember or recollect about your self or past experience?

What did you appreciate about your self or your talents?


What did you envision for your future?

**While reviewing the letter...**

What stood out to you about what Life Coaching is?

What stood out to you about what Life Coaching isn't?

How might this information shape your own Life Coaching journey?

What about Life Coaching sounds interesting to you?

What about Life Coaching sounds like it might be easy for you?

What about Life Coaching sounds like it might be a challenge for you?

Does anything about Life Coaching remain confusing for you? If so, what is it? How might you address your confusion?

## Contemplation Letter # 3:
## On the Whos and Hows of Life Coaching

### While reading the letter...

What questions came up in your own mind?

What thoughts did you have?

What made you pause and ponder?

What do you want to know more about?

What do you want to look deeper into?

What feelings came up for you?

What positives did you remember or recollect about your self or past experience?

What did you appreciate about your self or your talents?


What did you envision for your future?

## While reviewing the letter...

What do you picture when you picture the average Life Coaching client?

What might your ideal Life Coaching client look like?

How might you find your ideal Life Coaching client?

What do you think of when you hear the question, "What would you like to do some thinking about today?" How does that question make you feel?

When was a time you gave appreciation in your life? What was that appreciation? How did that appreciation affect the other person? How did giving the appreciation make you feel?

When was a time you received appreciation in your life? What did you think when you received that appreciation? How did that appreciation make you feel?

What does your experience with appreciation, both in terms of giving it and receiving it, tell you about its role in life and in Life Coaching? Based on this knowledge, how might you use it in the future?

How do you define the term challenge?

When was a time you compassionately challenged someone in your life? What was the challenge? How did that challenge affect the other person? How did you feel about compassionately challenging someone else?

When was a time you were compassionately challenged by someone in your life? How did that challenge affect your thoughts? How did you feel about that challenge? What was the end result of that challenge and your response to it?

How do you define the term block?

When was a time you realized someone had a block in their path? What was that block? Did you address it? If so, what thoughts and feelings did you have about addressing it?

When was a time you realized you had a block in your path? What was that block? Did you address it? If so, what thoughts and feelings did you have about addressing it?

## Contemplation Letter # 4:
## On Types of Life Coaching and
## What May Be of Interest to You

### While reading the letter...

What questions came up in your own mind?

What thoughts did you have?

What made you pause and ponder?

What do you want to know more about?

What do you want to look deeper into?

What feelings came up for you?

What positives did you remember or recollect about your self or past experience?

What did you appreciate about your self or your talents?


What did you envision for your future?

## While reviewing the letter...

What focuses in Life Coaching had you already heard of?

What focuses in Life Coaching are new to you?

What branches of Life Coaching sound interesting to you? For what reasons?

What branches of Life Coaching do not sound interesting to you? For what reasons?

What focuses in Life Coaching might you want to look more into?

What plan do you have for yourself in doing this?

How might you recognize and appreciate the work you have put into Life Coaching so far?

## Contemplation Letter # 5:
## On Educational Opportunities in Life Coaching
## and Which One Is Right for You

**While reading the letter...**

What questions came up in your own mind?

What thoughts did you have?

What made you pause and ponder?

What do you want to know more about?

What do you want to look deeper into?

What feelings came up for you?

What positives did you remember or recollect about your self or past experience?

What did you appreciate about your self or your talents?


What did you envision for your future?

**While reviewing the letter...**

What stands out to you about degree programs in Life Coaching?

What are the pros as you see them?

What are the cons as you see them?

How might a degree in Life Coaching fit in your life?

What stands out to you about certificate programs in Life Coaching?

What are the pros as you see them?

What are the cons as you see them?

How might a certificate in Life Coaching fit in your life?

What are the most important factors to you in choosing an educational track in Life Coaching?

What factors can you be more flexible with?

## Contemplation Letter # 6:
## On Further Credentialing in Life Coaching
## and How to Navigate the Alphabet Soup

### While reading the letter...

What questions came up in your own mind?

What thoughts did you have?

What made you pause and ponder?

What do you want to know more about?

What do you want to look deeper into?

What feelings came up for you?

What positives did you remember or recollect about your self or past experience?

What did you appreciate about your self or your talents?


What did you envision for your future?

## While reviewing the letter...

What stands out to you about the ICF individual credentialing options?

Are you interested in any of them? If so, which one or ones? For what reason(s)?

What timeline are you considering for pursuing your first ICF credential?

What is your plan for getting there?

What stands out to you about the IAC certification options?

Are you interested in any of them? If so, which one or ones? For what reason(s)?

What timeline are you considering for pursuing your first IAC certification?

What is your plan for getting there?

Are you familiar with any other credentialing options? If so, which ones? If not, are you planning on doing further research in this area?

How did it feel to read about so many different options?

What self-care did you engage in after reading the letter, if any?

## Determination Letter # 1:
## On Making Your Decision: To Be
## or Not to Be an Official Young Life Coach

### While reading the letter...

What questions came up in your own mind?

What thoughts did you have?

What made you pause and ponder?

What do you want to know more about?

What do you want to look deeper into?

What feelings came up for you?

What positives did you remember or recollect about your self or past experience?

What did you appreciate about your self or your talents?


What did you envision for your future?

**While reviewing the letter...**

What stands out to you about decisions in general?

What methods can you recall you've used to make decisions in the past?

Is there a method you've used before that seems like it fits with your Life Coach decision?

What past successful decisions can you recall having made?

How might such decisions and their processes help guide you through this one?

What are the pros for you when it comes to becoming a Life Coach?

What are the cons?

What kind of time do you want to give yourself to make this decision?


What are your feelings surrounding this decision?


Is there anyone you want to discuss this with? Who? When might you want to have this discussion?

## Determination Letter # 2:
## On Revealing Your Decision

### While reading the letter...

What questions came up in your own mind?

What thoughts did you have?

What made you pause and ponder?

What do you want to know more about?

What do you want to look deeper into?

What feelings came up for you?

What positives did you remember or recollect about your self or past experience?

What did you appreciate about your self or your talents?

What did you envision for your future?

## While reviewing the letter...

What did you decide? Are you going to become an official Young Life Coach? Or are you always going to carry a little bit of Life Coach with you?

How do you feel about your decision?

How does this decision affect the vision you have for your future?

What have you learned from your Life Coaching journey so far?

What lessons will you be taking to your next life stage?

How challenging was making the decision for you?

Did you use more time than you predicted to make the decision? Were you spot on with your prediction? Or did you use less?

What feelings did you have to sit with?

What feelings are present with you now?

What do you plan to address before you take your next life step? When might that be?

## Determination Letter # 3:
## On Reviewing Your Decision and
## Preparing for the Next Step

### While reading the letter...

What questions came up in your own mind?

What thoughts did you have?

What made you pause and ponder?

What do you want to know more about?

What do you want to look deeper into?

What feelings came up for you?

What positives did you remember or recollect about your self or past experience?

What did you appreciate about your self or your talents?


What did you envision for your future?

## While reviewing the letter...

What is it like to know you are going to become an official Life Coach?

What factors were the biggest contributors to your yes?

What factors did you have to plan around or overcome that tried to point you toward no?

Who have you told about your decision? How have they reacted?

How have you celebrated your decision?

What more would you like to record at this moment to capture this mindset?

What more would you like to record at this moment to capture your heartset?

## Action Letter # 1:
## On Setting Out to Become a Life Coach, The Effects It Will Have, and What You Are Looking Forward To

**While reading the letter...**

What questions came up in your own mind?

What thoughts did you have?

What made you pause and ponder?

What do you want to know more about?

What do you want to look deeper into?

What feelings came up for you?

What positives did you remember or recollect about your self or past experience?

What did you appreciate about your self or your talents?

What did you envision for your future?

**While reviewing the letter...**

What do you anticipate you might have to balance alongside Life Coaching?


What is your plan for making this happen?


What do you anticipate you might have to pause for now?


What is your plan for getting reacquainted with that when the time comes?


What do you anticipate you might have to say goodbye to?


How to you plan to adjust to that change?


Is there anything that you have already had to say goodbye to?

How have you handled that?

How do you typically navigate goodbyes?

How do you typically navigate hellos?

Is there anything you are saying hello to alongside Life Coaching?

What has that been like?

What additional thoughts might you like to chronicle right now?

What additional feelings might you like to capture?

**Action Letter # 2:
On Training's Beginning and
Your Chosen Path of Education**

## While reading the letter...

What questions came up in your own mind?

What thoughts did you have?

What made you pause and ponder?

What do you want to know more about?

What do you want to look deeper into?

What feelings came up for you?

What positives did you remember or recollect about your self or past experience?

What did you appreciate about your self or your talents?


What did you envision for your future?

**While reviewing the letter...**

Which pathway of education have you chosen?

What particular program?

What are the time commitments?

What are the money commitments?

How do you plan to meet these?

What do you know about yourself as a learner?

How have you best succeeded at learning in the past?

What do you want to bring forward from your previous learning successes?

Are there any challenges you face when learning?

How can you best overcome these?

What are you most looking forward to as part of the learning process?

## Action Letter # 3:
## On Your Mid-Training Check-In and
## Your Growth During the Educational Process

### While reading the letter...

What questions came up in your own mind?

What thoughts did you have?

What made you pause and ponder?

What do you want to know more about?

What do you want to look deeper into?

What feelings came up for you?

What positives did you remember or recollect about your self or past experience?

What did you appreciate about your self or your talents?

What did you envision for your future?

## While reviewing the letter...

What books have you read thus far?

What has been your favorite? What did you learn from it?

Do you have a favorite lecture? What made it special?

Do you have a favorite training experience? How did it impact you? What did you learn from it?

What skills has practice revealed that you brought with you to the Life Coaching table?

What skills are you learning that you want to keep close?

What positive feedback have you received about your abilities?

What have you been challenged to improve?

How has this process been for you? How are you adjusting?

Where and from whom have you been getting your support? Is there any additional support that you require? How do you plan to secure this for yourself?

## Action Letter # 4:
## On The End of Your Training Journey,
## At Least For Now, and What You Have Learned

**While reading the letter...**

What questions came up in your own mind?

What thoughts did you have?

What made you pause and ponder?

What do you want to know more about?

What do you want to look deeper into?

What feelings came up for you?

What positives did you remember or recollect about your self or past experience?

What did you appreciate about your self or your talents?

What did you envision for your future?

## While reviewing the letter...

What comes to mind as your favorite accomplishment in training?

Your favorite lesson?

Do you find your educational process was what you expected?

What surprised you in a positive way?

Was there anything you wished for that you didn't get?

What is your current vision of your Life Coaching future?

Have you had any more thoughts about the clients you want to work with in general?

Have you had any more thoughts about what branches or niches you would like to focus on in general?

How do your current musings differ from those you had at the very start of this journey?

What does this mean for the next leg of your Life Coaching journey?

## Action Letter # 5:
## On Goal Setting for Your Life Coaching Business:
## The First Round After Graduation

### While reading the letter...

What questions came up in your own mind?

What thoughts did you have?

What made you pause and ponder?

What do you want to know more about?

What do you want to look deeper into?

What feelings came up for you?

What positives did you remember or recollect about your self or past experience?

What did you appreciate about your self or your talents?

What did you envision for your future?

**While reviewing the letter...**

What goals come up as ones you want to set?

What is one big thing you would like to accomplish in Life Coaching?

What are the steps you must take to get there?

What are the associated timelines?

What is your current action plan?

Are there goals in other life areas that have been inspired by or relate to your Life Coaching journey? What are they?

What are the steps you must take to accomplish these?

And the associated timelines?

What is your first action step? When will you be taking it?

What is your favorite way to set goals and to track them?

What would your perfect day as a Life Coach look like?

What does this teach you about what you want?

What does this teach you about the path you will take to get there?

What has your imagined older, wiser self shown you?

What do you plan to do with those glimpses?

What do you find is most important to you in terms of your values?

How can you stay true to those during this portion of your journey?

## Action Letter # 6:
## On Goal Setting for Your Life Coaching Business:
## Finalizing Your Beginning Business Plan

### While reading the letter...

What questions came up in your own mind?

What thoughts did you have?

What made you pause and ponder?

What do you want to know more about?

What do you want to look deeper into?

What feelings came up for you?

What positives did you remember or recollect about your self or past experience?

What did you appreciate about your self or your talents?

What did you envision for your future?

**While reviewing the letter...**

Who do you picture as your ideal client?

What makes this type of client ideal for you?

What are the basic goals of this client?

How do you see yourself being of service to this client?

How do you plan to refer out clients who are not a good fit for you or whom you do not have the proper training to work with?

How does the idea of having to do this sit with you?

Will you be joining or creating a network of Life Coaching professionals? If so, how?

What manner of contact do you wish to have with them?

What kind of support would you like for them to provide to you?

What kind of support do you see yourself providing to them?

Do you have or are you planning on finding a Life Coach to work with?

What do you plan to work on with this Life Coach in regard to your Life Coaching venture?

Where might you provide Life Coaching services?

How many hours would you like to work each week?

How many of those are client contact hours?

How many do you see being devoted to other things? What kinds of things?

What figures do you have in mind related to your overhead? What additional information must you collect in order to guarantee financial success?

What are you seeking to make in your first year of Life Coaching? Your second? Your third?

How big do you see your business growing?

When will you know you business is big enough for you?

## Action Letter # 7:
## On Starting Your Life Coaching Business

### While reading the letter...

What questions came up in your own mind?

What thoughts did you have?

What made you pause and ponder?

What do you want to know more about?

What do you want to look deeper into?

What feelings came up for you?

What positives did you remember or recollect about your self or past experience?

What did you appreciate about your self or your talents?

What did you envision for your future?

**While reviewing the letter...**

How long has your business been open?

What about your business is as you predicted?

What about your business is different than you imagined?

In what ways have you had to adapt?

What feelings came up for you as you navigated such necessary change?

What further goals do you have for your business at this stage?

What timelines are attached to these?

What method do you have for checking in with yourself about the progress of your business?

What are you most proud of so far?

What are you most eager to work on next?

How are you chronicling these young days in your business?

## Action Letter # 8:
## On Compromising in the Name of Success
## and Holding On to What is Most Important

### While reading the letter...

What questions came up in your own mind?

What thoughts did you have?

What made you pause and ponder?

What do you want to know more about?

What do you want to look deeper into?

What feelings came up for you?

What positives did you remember or recollect about your self or past experience?

What did you appreciate about your self or your talents?


What did you envision for your future?

## While reviewing the letter...

What has been your most significant success so far?

What positives have resulted from it?

What has been your most challenging compromise so far?

What positives have resulted from it?

What appreciations have you offered yourself?

What have you celebrated?

What do you find you seek now?

Is there a new side you would like to add to your Life Coaching business?

Is there a change you would like to make to your existing services?

Is there a type of client or niche you find you are not presently suited for or passionate about?

Are there any expansions in your future?

Do you have handouts or materials you would like to create?

Are there any technological platforms you wish to access in order to expand or promote your business?

How do you now plan to continually check in with your goals, dreams, and accomplishments?

## Renewal Letter:
## On Checking In, Making Changes,
## and Self-Actualizing

### While reading the letter...

What questions came up in your own mind?

What thoughts did you have?

What made you pause and ponder?

What do you want to know more about?

What do you want to look deeper into?

What feelings came up for you?

What positives did you remember or recollect about your self or past experience?

What did you appreciate about your self or your talents?


What did you envision for your future?

## While reviewing the letter...

How do you see yourself as a Life Coach now?

What are your top five strengths?

What are some areas you would like to work on?

How might you address these?

Is there something new you would like to become involved with?

Is there something old that you want to become reacquainted with?

How is your relationship with your beginner's mind? Is there anything you want to work on there?

How is your relationship with your curious nature? Is there anything you would like to address in this area?

What is your current vision for your best self?

How does Life Coaching fit into this?

Where are you in terms of self-actualization?

In what ways have you self-actualized before?

How did you achieve these feats?

In what ways do you still wish to self-actualize?

How do you see yourself reaching these peaks?

What is the new version of your perfect day?


What is your new wiser self telling you that you must hear?


What passion is next?

## Maintenance Letter:
## On Keeping Up with New Goals,
## Always Being Flexible, and Remaining Forever Young

**While reading the letter...**

What questions came up in your own mind?

What thoughts did you have?

What made you pause and ponder?

What do you want to know more about?

What do you want to look deeper into?

What feelings came up for you?

What positives did you remember or recollect about your self or past experience?

What did you appreciate about your self or your talents?

What did you envision for your future?

**While reviewing the letter...**

What life areas underwent change as part of your renewal process?

What did the renewal process teach you in general?

How do you see renewal playing out in the rest of your life?

What must you focus on now in order to maintain your gains?

What resources do you need in order to succeed in this phase?

What successes from your past are you using to inspire yourself now?

How has this part of the cycle felt for you?

What are you most dedicated to now?

What are the values that guided you during this process?


How have your values helped you stay true to who you are and what you want?

## Legacy Letter:
## On Eternal Youth, Contributions to the Field,
## and Giving to Other Young Life Coaches

### While reading the letter...

What questions came up in your own mind?

What thoughts did you have?

What made you pause and ponder?

What do you want to know more about?

What do you want to look deeper into?

What feelings came up for you?

What positives did you remember or recollect about your self or past experience?

What did you appreciate about your self or your talents?

What did you envision for your future?

**While reviewing the letter...**

What do you see as your legacy?

What unique gifts do you think you provided to your clients just by being you?

What moments are most memorable across your career?

In what way do you think you helped other Life Coaches?

What is your favorite among your many contributions?

How do you think you and your life benefitted from your career as a Life Coach?

What is the best gift Life Coaching gave you?

For what experience do you have the most gratitude?


How do you plan to celebrate your career?


What do you wish to do next?

## Closing Letter:
## On Good Luck, Not Goodbye

**While reading the letter...**

What questions came up in your own mind?

What thoughts did you have?

What made you pause and ponder?

What do you want to know more about?

What do you want to look deeper into?

What feelings came up for you?

What positives did you remember or recollect about your self or past experience?

What did you appreciate about your self or your talents?

What did you envision for your future?

**While reviewing the letter...**

What stands out most about your Life Coaching journey?

What makes the path you have taken uniquely yours?

How do you define your self now?

In what way does the above definition differ from how you defined your self at the beginning of your Life Coaching journey?

How can you recognize when you are being your best self?

How does it feel to be your best self?

What is your favorite word from the happiness category?

How do you plan to stay in touch with that feeling as part of your Life Coaching process?


How do you plan to stay in touch with that feeling as part of your life journey?


What closing words do you have for yourself now?


How does it feel to have these letters end?


How does it feel to be wished good luck instead of goodbye?


How has your confidence grown as part of this process?

# THE POST SCRIPTS

## Common Concepts

This section includes  a list of common concepts found within Life Coaching and the Life Coaching literature. Each entry includes the identified word, a definition of the word, further thoughts on the word, related terms and/or phrases, and a reference to where the term first appears in the book.

Each common concept appears in bold for easy identification. A chosen concept is one that can be found either in its exact form across Life Coaching texts or as a similar or related term.

The definition of a concept is an explanation of the included word in basic terms. Each definition is meant to distill the common concept to its simplest form.

Further thoughts on a word involve an enhanced exploration of the term based on its use within Life Coaching. The purpose of this enhanced exploration is to provide additional clarification of what the term means, demonstrate how the term relates to a coaching conversation, and help create a solid foundation of knowledge for the Young Life Coach. When gender specific pronouns are used to elaborate on a concept, they are alternated. Thus, the use of the word she with one concept is followed by the use of the word he with another. This is to promote readability as well as to demonstrate that both men and women make use of Life Coaching. In some cases, both the coach and client will be assigned gender specific pronouns. In this case, the coach's gender and client's gender will differ so it is clear who is who.

Related terms and phrases have been included in order to provide a simple reference to the listed concept as well as to build bridges between different though related terms found within the Life Coaching literature.

First appearances of a word are italicized within a letter. The first identified appearance of a word is restricted to either the exact word used to identify the common concept or a pluralized form of the word. Related words are not considered a first appearance and may be found prior to the first identified entry of a word. For example, the word connect can be found in several forms prior to its first appearance: connected, reconnect, connector. First appearances are listed by letter, paragraph within a letter, and sentence within a paragraph for easy reference.

## Accountability

Definition – The state of holding oneself responsible for one's life and life choices

Further Thoughts: In Life Coaching, accountability involves both you the coach and the client. The client's role is to identify life areas to work on, explore related thoughts and feelings, generate potential options for action, select from among preferred choices, create specific plans and concrete goals, commit to plans, work toward goals, recognize efforts made, acknowledge accomplishments, and identify opportunities for future improvement. By doing this, the client ensures she is an active participant throughout the accountability process thereby demonstrating that she is serious about creating the life she wants.

Your role as the coach is to facilitate client accountability. You can achieve this by supporting the client through the coaching conversation, tracking what the client wants to work on, checking in with efforts and gains, and modeling accountability by staying engaged in the coaching process. In this way, you are communicating that you take the client's dreams and wishes seriously. It is often by demonstrating that you have bought in to the coaching process that you secure and enhance the client's own buy-in, which is a significant part of coaching effectiveness.

Related Terms/Phrases:
Commitment
Responsibility

First Appearance: Fifth sentence in the sixteenth paragraph of Contemplation Letter 6. Contemplation Letter 6 opens with, "You may be wondering, 'How many choices....'" The sixteenth paragraph begins, "Masteries refers to the fact...." The fifth sentence starts, "Plan means the ideas being submitted are...." (p. 17)

## Act of Life

Definition – Phase of existence

Further Thoughts: In Life Coaching, life can be said to be broken down into three phases, much like a play. The first act of life is defined by a person's birth and growth into the person he is to become. The second act is defined as the choice of a life focus, which is often either related to career or the start of a family, and which defines the person's purpose. The third act refers to the events that occur after the resolution of the second act, typically marked by children leaving home or retirement.

Many life coaches are said to enter the profession during their third act, though more and more individuals are adding Life Coaching to their present careers or using Life Coaching to support themselves financially while they raise children. Due to lengthening life spans and the different ways in which careers are approached now, with many shifts and changes across a lifespan now commonplace, it is possible to conceive of a life as having more than three acts.

In terms of the client, it is not uncommon for him to come to coaching during the transitions between acts. Retirement, particularly, is a time when people seek out coaching. Also, the client is likely to pursue services when he is making changes to his career.

Related Terms/Phrases:
Developmental Stage
Life Phase
Life Stage

First Appearance: First sentence in the eleventh paragraph of Contemplation Letter 1. Contemplation Letter 1 opens with, "Your journey to becoming a Life Coach…." The eleventh paragraph begins, "If you are in your first act of life…." The first sentence is the beginning of the eleventh paragraph and thus has the same start as the paragraph itself. (p. 6)

## Action Plan

Definition – A designed path for achieving a goal or set of goals

Further Thoughts: In Life Coaching, the client designs the action plan with the support of you the coach. An action plan, in its most basic form, includes goals and an identified way to achieve them. Goals are often divided into larger, long-term pursuits and smaller, short-term pursuits. Time frames for completion tend to vary, with short-term goals placed on a daily, weekly, or monthly time line and long-term goals placed on a multiple-month, yearly, or multiple-year time line. Goals are often spelled out in precise language so that achievement is easily identifiable.

The client's role is to think about and discuss what goals she wants to pursue, decide how to pursue them, and follow through on the commitments she makes. This puts her at the center of the action plan and its creation. Your role as the coach is to reflect back what you hear, help the client achieve success, and check in to make sure that the pledges she makes are being honored with effort that results in progress.

Related Terms/Phrases:
Approach
Game Plan
Goal
Program
S.M.A.R.T. Goals
Strategy

First Appearance: Fifth sentence in the sixteenth paragraph of Contemplation Letter 6. Contemplation Letter 6 opens with, "You may be wondering, 'How many choices....'" The sixteenth paragraph begins, "Masteries refers to the fact...." The fifth sentence starts, "Plan means the ideas being submitted are...." (p. 17)

## Appreciation

Definition – Recognition offered by one person to another

Further Thoughts: In Life Coaching, appreciation often takes the form of positive verbal feedback provided by you the coach to the client about the client's thoughts, feelings, behaviors, character traits, or progress toward goals. It can also be demonstrated via nonverbal means such as by maintaining steady eye contact, facing the client, keeping distracting body movements to a minimum, and using a purposeful facial expression, such as a smile.

Due to the collaborative nature of Life Coaching, the client can also demonstrate appreciation to you for your work as a coach. Overt demonstrations of appreciation by the client are often verbal. Giving thanks and underscoring the usefulness of an approach or tool in promoting thinking are the most common forms. The client can also show his appreciation for your efforts in more subtle ways including by fully engaging in the coaching conversation, being open and curious, challenging himself to expand his thinking, and following through on homework and other chosen tasks of accountability. In your journey as a coach, you will find, though the client engages your services as a coach for the purpose of pursuing his dreams, he shows appreciation for himself, for you, and the Life Coaching process by achieving what he most wishes to achieve.

As part of his role, the client most frequently shows his appreciation through constant and purposeful engagement in the process. You will, as part of your role as the coach, consistently support this engagement, including by verbalizing what is most appreciated about the client's efforts and progress. By doing this, you are assisting the client in creating a template for how to achieve such gains in the future. You are also helping the client to connect to what makes him special.

Related Terms/Phrases:
Acknowledgement
Affirmation
Belief
Recognition
Interest

First Appearance: First sentence in the fifth paragraph of the Pre-Contemplation Letter. The Pre-Contemplation Letter opens with, "You might be wondering why...." The fifth paragraph begins, "This appreciation of self...." The first sentence is the beginning of the fifth paragraph and thus has the same start as the paragraph itself. (p. 4)

## Approach

Definition – A plan, strategy, or method

Further Thoughts: In Life Coaching, approaches are often focused on the general process as well as the smaller steps used to achieve success.

Your role as the coach is to decide what approach is most in line with your values and training as a coach as well as what methods are most effective for the client at hand. Though a certain commitment to how to do things is a natural part of your identity as a coach, it is important that you remain flexible and willing to grow. This models for the client the importance of adaptation in her own life.

The client's role is to become familiar with the general approach used in coaching as well as to understand the methods by which her success is being supported and achieved. This requires deep listening and a willingness to ask questions in order to become informed, clarify an unknown, or enhance the implementation and effectiveness of a strategy.

Related Terms/Phrases:
Method
Orientation
Theory

First Appearance: In plural form. Second sentence in the seventh paragraph of Contemplation Letter 2. Contemplation Letter 2 opens with, "Your mind may be filled with thoughts…." The seventh paragraph begins with, "On the other hand, are you looking…." The second sentence starts, "Do you have more knowledge…." (p. 7)

## Assessment

Definition – A tool used to gather information and form an opinion; also the act of gathering information and forming an opinion

Further Thoughts: In Life Coaching, assessments come in all shapes and sizes. The most common assessment used in Life Coaching is an intake. The word intake describes the portion of the Welcome Packet that asks the client to provide background information as well as a current picture of himself and what he wants to work on. The intake also refers to the first session in which you as the coach review the limits of confidentiality, become acquainted with the client, and gather background information pertinent to the reason you were hired.

The role of the client in assessment is to participate and provide information so that what is gleaned can enhance both your understanding of him and his understanding of himself as well as his life situation. Your role as the coach is to choose the appropriate measures or create them, as in the case of the intake. You must also interpret any findings and incorporate them into your larger understanding of the person you are helping. In the case of some assessments, you might need to seek out additional training or stay abreast of updates.

As a coach, it is important that you understand that assessments are only meant to assist you in getting to know the client. They neither provide a whole nor unalterable picture of the person you are working with.

Related Terms/Phrases:
Intake
Test
Tool
Measure
Welcome Packet

First Appearance: Fourth sentence in the seventh paragraph of Contemplation Letter 6. Contemplation Letter 6 opens with, "You may be wondering, 'How many choices….'" The seventh paragraph begins with, "The Associate Certified Coach…." The fourth sentence starts, "The core components are training received…." (p. 15)

## Authentic

Definition – True, real

Further Thoughts: In Life Coaching, being authentic is both a requirement for the process to work and an aim of the journey. The role of the client is to be her true self. She can accomplish this by sharing her true thoughts, feelings, and approaches to life (behaviors).

Your role as the coach is to recognize and support the client's steps in being authentic. This may take the form of validation and affirmation or it may take the form of challenging information that doesn't fit with what you know about the client.

In order to ensure that the Thinking Space is an authentic space, you, too, must be authentic as the coach. For the most part, this involves engaging with the client in a meaningful way by deeply listening, asking powerful questions, helping to create accountability measures, and assisting with the design of action plans. However, being authentic can also include you being willing to share pieces of yourself and your experience that aid the process and that are in the best interest of the client.

Related Terms/Phrases:
Identity
Real
Self
True

First Appearance: Third sentence in the fourth Paragraph of the Closing Letter. The Closing Letter opens with, "In closing, I find I want to make…." The fourth paragraph begins, "Be to yourself what you are…." The third sentence is, "Be authentic." (p. 48)

## Awareness

Definition – Knowledge or perception of a fact, person, process, or situation

Further Thoughts: In Life Coaching, awareness is a constant. It is the foundation from which coaching starts and the aim of any and all measures undertaken. The client comes to coaching because he is aware that he wants more – more from his life and more for himself. His role is to share this awareness and what it means to him as well as to work on deepening his knowledge and understanding of himself, his values, his goals, and his dreams.

Your role as the coach is to be aware of what is said and what isn't said, to catch what is verbalized and to use your knowledge of body language, voice tone and volume, and word choice to enhance your understanding of what is being shared. Your role is also to promote your client's understanding of himself, his life, people, processes, and the world, including his place in it.

Related Terms/Phrases:
Engagement
Interest
Knowledge
Mindful
Perspective
Relationship to

First Appearance: Second sentence in the fifth paragraph of Determination Letter 1. Determination Letter 1 opens with, "Now is the tricky part." The fifth paragraph begins with, "You may, after the pause, find you are...." The second sentence starts, "You may have, in your conscious awareness...." (p. 19)

## Balance

Definition – A state of equilibrium

Further Thoughts: In Life Coaching, balance often refers to the intellectual and emotional equilibrium achieved by a client when the appropriate time, attention, resources, and effort are dedicated to life areas identified as important. The client's role is to listen to her own thoughts, pay attention to her feelings, and use the two to prioritize what she most wants.

Your role as the coach is to believe that what the client says is important actually is and to support her on her journey to inner harmony. You may also reflect upon observations of the client's shared thoughts, confided feelings, and demonstrated behaviors, in their individual form or as collective patterns, in order to bring to the client's awareness things that are integral to her attainment of wellness, meaning, and joy.

Related Terms/Phrases:
Equilibrium
Equity
Give equal weight to
Harmony

First Appearance: First sentence in the second paragraph of Action Letter 1. Action Letter 1 opens with, "With each new addition to your life…." The second paragraph begins, "What do you anticipate you might…." The first sentence is the beginning of the second paragraph and thus has the same start as the paragraph itself. (p. 24)

## Beginner's Mind

Definition – A mental state in which a person approaches what is being heard or learned as though it is brand new

Further Thoughts: In Life Coaching, you the coach are charged with approaching the coaching conversation and the client's thinking with a beginner's mind. This means you must adopt an intellectual state in which you are open to new information, eager to learn more, and willing to approach what is being transmitted without prejudgment or preconception.

Through the coaching process, the client is also invited to adopt a beginner's mind. The client can accomplish this by approaching his own thoughts and feelings with curiosity and impartiality. Together, you and the client can discover new perspectives on what is being discussed and routes for helping the client secure what he wants.

Related Terms/Phrases:
Curious
Impartial
Open-minded

First Appearance: Third sentence in the fourth paragraph of the Introduction Letter. The Introduction Letter opens with, "Somehow this book has found its way…." The fourth paragraph begins, "I welcome you…." The third sentence starts, "That is one of coaching's many gifts…." (p. 3)

## Beginning

Definition – The start of the Life Coaching session during which previously assigned homework is checked in with and the focus of the day's conversation is decided; also, the start of the Life Coaching relationship

Further Thoughts: In Life Coaching, the beginning of the session sets the stage for the remainder of the coaching conversation. During the beginning of the session, the client frequently reports on previously assigned homework, shares recent updates, and identifies what she would like to talk about for the day.

At this stage, your role as the coach is to listen intently to what is shared. On occasion, you may need to ask key questions in order to help the client decipher what she most wants to discuss. This is especially true when the client's head is overcrowded with thoughts or when she has put forth numerous topics as possibilities for further exploration. You may also have to assist the client in moving from reporting about her life to thinking more deeply about herself and her circumstances. This shift marks the transition from the beginning of the session to the middle, where the majority of the work is done.

The client's role is to come prepared to talk and to participate in the session. The client may find she can benefit from filling out a session preparation form, often provided by the coach. This can assist her in whittling down what is most important for her to discuss. Also, the client must be honest about homework, whether or not she has completed it. If any issues in completing the homework exist, the beginning of the session is the time to troubleshoot them and formulate a new approach so that consistent work is done between coaching conversations.

In the beginning of the Life Coaching relationship, your role is to introduce the client to coaching, including reviewing the limits of confidentiality and your role as a coach, as well as to assist the client in discovering why she wants to pursue that which she does. The client's role is to approach the start of coaching by being open, honest, and willing to grow and learn.

Related Terms/Phrases:
Opening
Start
Update

First Appearance: Fourth sentence in the ninth paragraph of Action Letter 4. Action Letter 4 opens with, "You are graduating from training...." The ninth paragraph begins, "Would a visualization...." The fourth sentence starts, "Can you imagine what your ideal...." (p. 30)

## Behavior

Definition – Manner of conduct; response to stimuli or the environment

Further Thoughts: In Life Coaching, thoughts are seen as antecedents to behavior. They are the point at which behavior can best be influenced.

Your role as the coach is to help the client understand the relationship between his thoughts, feelings, and behaviors. The general setup of this relationship is something that is often introduced early in the relationship. Checking in with this relationship is done throughout coaching, sometimes in a formal way and sometimes more informally. Formal check-ins include using specific strategies to explain and explore behavior that are supported by the theory or theories you use to guide your work and your sessions.

The role of the client is to disclose significant thoughts, feelings, and behaviors, especially in terms of selected goals, so that progress and the effectiveness of progress can be better understood. Through exploration of these thoughts, feelings, and behaviors, stumbling blocks and limitations can be identified and addressed.

Related Terms/Phrases:
A-B-C Model
Belief
Cognitive-Behavioral Coaching
Feeling
Limiting Belief
Thought

First Appearance: Seventh sentence in the second paragraph of Action Letter 4. Action Letter 4 opens with, "You are graduating from training…." The second paragraph begins, "Are you still anxiously exploring…." The seventh sentence starts, "Have you found, as so many do…." (p. 30)

## Being

Definition – The state of engagement with life, especially the present

Further Thoughts: In Life Coaching, being is the ultimate goal for both you the coach and the client. At the start of the coaching relationship, the client is learning to do the things that will help her achieve success. Later, as she becomes more comfortable with the process and the skills she has learned have time to settle in as habits, she will naturally do the things that will be of benefit to her. In this way, she is being the change. She is being herself – her new self.

You, too, as a coach will go through a similar journey. At first, you do what you are supposed to do as a coach. You acclimatize the client to the process, you use legal and ethical guidelines to make appropriate decisions, you rely on your knowledge of strategies to address the issues at hand, etc. Later, these things become natural to you. There is less of a need to concentrate on the decision-making process and more of a requirement to allow yourself to use your now educated intuition. The manner in which you engage with the client before you depends on where you are in your own journey. The longer you work in the field and the more comfortable you become with coaching, the more being is present in your work and the less you need to focus on doing.

Related Terms/Phrases:
Embodying
Living the Lesson
Walking the Walk

First Appearance: Fifth sentence in the eleventh paragraph of Action Letter 8. Action Letter 8 opens with, "How are things going?" The eleventh paragraph begins, "Do they include adding...." The fifth sentence starts, "Maybe exploring how...." (p. 39)

## Belief

Definition – Interest or faith shown in another; conviction

Further Thoughts: In Life Coaching, belief is an integral part of the process. To start, you as the coach must believe in the process. You must believe in your abilities as a professional. You must also believe in the client. This means you have faith that the process works, that you can help the client through the use of coaching's tenets, and that the client is coachable and able to achieve his dreams with a little support and help.

Your role as the coach is to embody this belief from the beginning of the relationship to the end, from the start of the session until its conclusion. Whereas being open and curious is desirable and helpful, doubting is not. It is through the strength of your conviction that you turn coaching into a belief-engendering process. If you begin to experience doubt, either in the process, your abilities, or the client, it is incumbent upon you to secure the support you need. Common ways you can seek support as the coach are scheduling a mentoring session, checking in with a colleague, spending time with a member of your support network, or engaging in self-care.

The client's role is to be open to the coaching process and to be willing to deepen his appreciation and respect for himself and his abilities. The client will often voice doubt, either in himself, the relevance of his goals, or his ability to reach his dreams; this is an invitation for you, the coach, to help him restore his faith and trust in himself.

Related Terms/Phrases:
Belief-Engendering
Faith
Hope

First Appearance: First sentence in the eleventh paragraph of Action Letter 4. Action Letter 4 opens with, "You are graduating from training…." The eleventh paragraph begins, "Transitioning from learning to doing…." The first sentence is the beginning of the eleventh paragraph and thus has the same start as the paragraph itself. (p. 30)

## Block

Definition – Obstacle

Further Thoughts: In Life Coaching, blocks, also known as stumbling blocks, are the most common and frequent impediments to progress. Frequently, blocks come in the form of limiting thoughts or beliefs that lead a client to move from can-do thinking to can't-do thinking. These thoughts can take the form of beliefs about self, others, life, or the world. Such thoughts are often rigid and contain judgment, resulting in a template full of right ways and wrong ways to do things or be.

Your role as the coach is to help the client uncover blocks to progress, no matter what their form. In order to remove blocks, they must first be named, then defined, then explored, then challenged, then overcome. By listening to the client, you will often find that an insurmountable obstacle in the client's eyes inspires several solutions in yours. It is your job to teach the client to think around these obstacles and, thus, free her mind.

The client's role in identifying and overcoming blocks is to be honest about hitches in progress and challenges to belief. Many limiting beliefs are formed in childhood and are, thus, not in the client's everyday awareness. They tend to come to the surface in the form of doubts or feeling stuck. Thus, when your client reports she feels stuck or doesn't think she can do something, there exists a perfect opportunity for you and she to explore the blocks that have her feeling that way.

Related Terms/Phrases:
Challenge
Hurdle
Obstacle
Opportunity
Stumbling Block

First Appearance: Fourth sentence in the seventh paragraph of Contemplation Letter 3. Contemplation Letter 3 opens with, "At this stage, you may be wondering...." The seventh paragraph begins, "Challenging can happen...." The fourth sentence starts, "It isn't muscle or magic...." (p. 9)

## Boundary

Definition – Something that identifies or sets a limit

Further Thoughts: In Life Coaching, boundaries are a natural part of the process. You as the coach start the process of coaching by defining what it is and isn't coaching, delineating the topics you do and do not work with, explaining the limits of confidentiality, and going over your expectations of the client. All of these activities are forms of boundary setting. You will also help the client redefine boundaries throughout the process through the expansion of techniques that do work and the erasure of approaches that don't.

The client sets boundaries by deciding what he wants to work on, by disclosing that which is pertinent, and by helping decide upon home-work and means of accountability (including saying no to approaches that are not for him). The client may also set boundaries through simple preferences such as only wanting to have coaching sessions at the beginning or end of a week or preferring morning coaching calls to those in the afternoon.

Related Terms/Phrases:
Holding Your Ground
Limit
Saying No

First Appearance: In plural form. Fifth sentence in the nineteenth paragraph of the Renewal Letter. The Renewal Letter opens with, "Having a Life Coaching business...." The nineteenth paragraph begins, "Or maybe you would like...." The fifth sentence starts, "To, via your example, help...." (p. 43)

## Calling

Definition – A strong inner pull towards a specific purpose, profession, or vocation; for those of faith, this inner pull is part of a connection to a Higher Power and related to that Higher Power's design

Further Thoughts: In Life Coaching, the client often comes to the process in search of a sense of purpose and the satisfaction that comes from engaging with and serving that purpose. The word calling is often a good descriptor for the biggest purpose the client has in the life area of work or volunteer/service activities. The client's role is to be open to the process of identifying and working toward a calling.

Your role as a coach is to help the client discover her purpose, often through the exploration and identification of values. Values are the whys behind the whats and hows, the reasons the client chooses to work toward those things that are important to her.

Related Terms/Phrases:
Destiny
Purpose
Role
Value

First Appearance: First sentence in the sixth paragraph of Action Letter 8. Action Letter 8 opens with, "How are things going?" The sixth paragraph begins, "I wonder if you can do that...." The first sentence is the beginning of the sixth paragraph and thus has the same start as the paragraph itself. (p. 38)

## Celebrate

Definition – To mark or honor an accomplishment or set of achievements

Further Thoughts: In Life Coaching, celebration is key. The client may come to the process unfamiliar with celebrating either himself or that which he has achieved. He may feel guilty for even thinking about honoring who he is or what he has done.

Therefore, it is your role as the coach to demonstrate the importance of celebration, one of the most significant functions of which is to inspire further achievement. Also, it is important for the client to know that effort is an important aspect of the process to celebrate not just the results. Putting in effort is the means by which results will come, but results are often dependent on circumstances and other factors outside of the client's control.

Related Terms/Phrases:
Acknowledge
Appreciate
Honor
Make Known

First Appearance: Eighth sentence in the seventh paragraph of Determination Letter 3. Determination Letter 3 opens with, "Congratulations! You are here." The seventh paragraph begins, "What is unique about your...." The eighth sentence starts, "How might you celebrate..." (p. 23)

## Challenge

Definition – To question the legitimacy of; to encourage to further explore

Further Thoughts: In Life Coaching, your role as the coach is to challenge the client when doing so is of benefit. You must always challenge with purpose and care. The goal of a challenge is often to have a client look more closely at whether or not a shared thought, assumed truth, or predicted consequence of an action is realistic.

Through being challenged by you, the client can learn to question her own thoughts, assumptions, and predictions. This helps the client get closer to her own truth and the truths of the world, which allows for decisions and actions to come from an authentic, reality-based place.

Related Terms/Phrases:
Compassionate edge
Confront

First Appearance: Second sentence in the seventh paragraph of Contemplation Letter 3. Contemplation Letter 3 opens with, "At this stage, you may be wondering…". The seventh paragraph begins, "Challenging can happen…." The second sentence starts, "A challenge that is honest…." (p. 9)

## Childlike

Definition – Marked by the enthusiasm, curiosity, and awe of childhood

Further Thoughts: In Life Coaching, you and the client are both charged with being childlike in various ways. Having a beginner's mind, being curious, pursuing joy, and engaging in play are just some of the ways being childlike is accomplished.

The client's role is to shed his self-consciousness and to fully engage in being his true self. Your role as the coach is both to model the importance of being childlike and to acknowledge, appreciate, and celebrate the client's accomplishment in assuming this approach.

Related Terms/Phrases:
Artless
Natural
True to Self

First Appearance: Fourth sentence in the eighteenth paragraph of the Renewal Letter. The Renewal Letter opens with, "Having a Life Coaching business…." The eighteenth paragraph begins, "Maybe you want to write…." The fourth sentence starts, "To illustrate the use of…." (p. 43)

## Clarify

Definition – To enhance understanding through the removal of confusion and uncertainty

Further Thoughts: In Life Coaching, to clarify is to ensure that a thought, feeling, behavior, or plan of action is well defined and understood, often through the use of questions and answers that eliminate ambiguity and confusion within a person or between people.

Your role in the clarification process as the coach is to start by listening to the client's thoughts and noting any points of incongruence revealed by her word choice, tone, facial expression, or body language. You can then name these observations in an effort to encourage the client to check in with herself and recognize the information she is sharing both verbally and nonverbally.

The client's role then becomes to further explore what she is thinking and any related feelings such thoughts produce. It is through several exchanges such as these that the client begins to weed out her true thoughts and feelings from those she thinks she should have or those that she has borrowed from others. Once the client is clear about what she thinks and believes, she is free to move toward pursuing her true goals and reaching for her authentic dreams.

Related Terms/Phrases:
Expand Upon
Fine-Tune
Solidify

First Appearance: Second sentence in the eighteenth paragraph of the Renewal Letter. The Renewal Letter opens with, "Having a Life Coaching business…." The eighteenth paragraph begins, "Maybe you want to write…." The second sentence starts, "To discuss the intricacies…." (p. 43)

## Clean Language

Definition – An approach to communication that facilitates the client's thinking without interference from the coach

Further Thoughts: In Life Coaching, your role as the coach is to facilitate the client's thinking and communication process. Your goal is to be an assistant in this process who helps further discovery. Therefore, when you communicate, it is important that you do not muddy the waters with your own thinking and speaking style. This, of course, is where clean language comes in.

Originally, much of clean language involved making sure you as the coach did not introduce your own metaphors and personal points of reference into the discussion. Over time, clean language has come to refer to any communication techniques used to allow the client full and unfettered access to sharing and expressing himself in the way he naturally would. This means you will refrain from introducing metaphors and examples of your own when it serves the best interest of the client. It also means you will use questions that are clear and make statements that are simple, effective, and on topic.

The client's role is to communicate in as natural a way as possible. The client's role is also to develop strategies over time that result in his shared thoughts being as close to his true ideas as possible.

Related Terms/Phrases:
Pure
True

First Appearance: Fourth sentence in the nineteenth paragraph of the Renewal Letter. The Renewal Letter opens with, "Having a Life Coaching business…." The nineteenth paragraph begins, "Or maybe you would like…." The fourth sentence starts, "To showcase the importance of…." (p. 43)

## Client

Definition – The person in the Life Coaching relationship who is receiving services

Further Thoughts: In Life Coaching, the client is responsible for making life choices. Though the coaching relationship is collaborative in nature, the client assumes full responsibility for decision-making and follow through. This is to ensure that the client is in the driver's seat of her life and remains empowered to create the life she wishes to create.

Your role as the coach is to support the client throughout the process by listening, providing feedback, challenging, and appreciating. Your presence as the coach with your listening mind leads the client to think and dream in ways she has not before.

Related Terms/Phrases:
Coachee
Thinker

First Appearance: In plural form. First sentence in the fourth paragraph of Pre-Contemplation Letter. Pre-Contemplation Letter opens with, "You might be wondering why...." Fourth paragraph begins, "Life Coaching clients...." The first sentence is the beginning of the fourth paragraph and thus has the same start as the paragraph itself. (p. 4)

## Close-Ended Question

Definition – Inquiries that can be answered with a yes or no

Further Thoughts: In Life Coaching, questions are used to further discussion and the client's understanding of himself and his goals and dreams. Therefore, close-ended questions are used sparingly.

Your role as a coach is to decide when to use close-ended questions, to determine when they will be most effective and will further the process rather than hinder it. Often, a close-ended question can be used in assessing accountability. For instance, if a client promised to spend one hour journaling on Friday night at 7:00 PM, you can ask, "Did you spend an hour on Friday at 7:00 PM journaling?" The answer to this is either yes or no. In fact, accountability measures are purposefully defined thoroughly so that any follow-up questions can easily determine whether the client remained true to his commitment or not.

The client's role is to answer close-ended questions honestly and to understand their purpose. They are not aimed at nailing the client for infractions, but often at holding him accountable.

Other close-ended questions are often used to clear the haze, such as, "Do you want to work on...," "Are you passionate about...," or "Is that something that is important to you?" The goal is to get around the hemming and hawing, the rigmarole that is often a stumbling block for the client.

Related Terms/Phrases:
Yes or No Question

First Appearance: In plural form. Second sentence in the nineteenth paragraph of the Renewal Letter. The Renewal Letter opens with, "Having a Life Coaching business...." The nineteenth paragraph begins, "Or maybe you would like...." The second sentence starts, "To show new coaches how...." (p. 43)

## Coachability

Definition – The state of being able to be coached and benefit from coaching

Further Thoughts: In Life Coaching, it is important to assess for a client's coachability. The first step in this process is to make sure the client wants coaching services. The two most commonly sought services that are confused with coaching are therapy and consulting. Therapy involves helping a person heal, often by addressing current dysfunctions; therapy also involves sorting through the past to understand how the present came to be. Consulting involves giving a person answers to specific questions about how to do things or addresses particular issues, often related to business endeavors.

If the client is determined to be in search of coaching services, the next step is to make sure she is ready for coaching. In short, this means that she must be in a place where she can benefit from the process. The biggest reason a client would not be able to benefit from the process early on would be because of a health issue that does not allow for adequate participation. Many of these prohibitory health issues come in the form of mental health issues. Having and using a referral guide is helpful for you as the coach here.

The other primary reason clients cannot or do not benefit from coaching is lack of commitment to and engagement in the process. This is something that often becomes apparent over time. Dishonesty and lack of follow through on homework are two of the biggest culprits.

Therefore, it comes as no surprise that the client's role in being coachable is to be clear about what services she is looking for and to be upfront and open in discussions as well as to complete coaching assignments.

If the client is determined to be inappropriate for coaching services at any point, it is your duty as the coach to communicate this to client in as tactful and compassionate a manner as possible.

Related Terms/Phrases:
Client Readiness

First Appearance: Second sentence in the eighteenth paragraph of the Renewal Letter. The Renewal Letter opens with, "Having a Life Coaching business...." The eighteenth paragraph begins, "Maybe you want to write...." The second sentence starts, "To discuss the intricacies...." (p. 43)

## Collaborate

Definition – The process by which two people work together as equals

Further Thoughts: In Life Coaching, you and the client work together as a team. Your shared goal is to create a space where the client can do his best thinking. Through optimal thinking, the client can uncover wants, identify dreams, create goals, and pursue the life he has always wanted to live. The client is responsible for bringing content to the session. You as the coach are responsible for assisting the client in delving deeper into himself to discover what can help him thrive.

As equals, you and the client are able to interact in a relaxed and authentic manner where each of you can appreciate the positive attributes of the other. It is through this beingness that coaching is said to assume its transformational power.

Related Terms/Phrases:
Ally
Cooperate
Join
Partner

First Appearance: First sentence in the third paragraph of Contemplation Letter 3. Contemplation Letter 3 opens with, "At this stage, you may be wondering…." The third paragraph begins, "Life Coaches work with others…." The first sentence is the beginning of the third paragraph and thus has the same start as the paragraph itself. (p. 9)

## Confidentiality

Definition – The state of being private or secret, often used to refer to the existence of the coaching relationship as well as the process's contents

Further Thoughts: In Life Coaching, confidentiality is something you offer the client. The client can talk freely about sessions as she sees fit. You as the coach can only reveal that the client is a client if given permission. Also, you can reveal what is discussed in sessions only if given permission. In coaching, unlike in therapy, the client is much more likely to be okay with others knowing she is receiving services.

Necessarily, confidentiality includes limits. One of the most common is ensuring that you neither aid nor abet the client's harm to self or others. Harm can come in the form of a direct threat to self or others either in the present or in the near future. It can also come in the form of a confession to abusing dependents, which include children or disabled or elderly persons who need care. These are things that must be reported to the proper authorities; the client must know the outcome of such disclosures at the start of a coaching relationship before anything is shared.

When discussing the limits of confidentiality, it is also essential that the client know that, though you can maintain confidentiality, you do not, as a coach, have any rights to privilege and can, therefore, be compelled to disclose the nature and content of coaching sessions if asked to do so by law enforcement or the courts. Due to the fact the laws vary between and across states, it is important to consult with an attorney to make sure you are properly disclosing limits to confidentiality in your intake paperwork.

Related Terms/Phrases:
Limits of Confidentiality
Privacy

First Appearance: Sixth sentence in the fifth paragraph of Action Letter 6. Action Letter 6 opens with, "By now, you have set a few goals...." The fifth paragraph begins, "Have you already identified people...." The sixth sentence starts, "The finer points of confidentiality...." (p. 34)

## Connect

Definition – The process by which one person joins with another in a conversation or interaction

Further Thoughts: In Life Coaching, your job as the coach is to connect with the client. In order to accomplish this, you must listen closely to what the client is saying as well as to what is not being said. You can use word choice, voice volume, tone, facial expression, and body language to improve your understanding of the client as a person. It is this understanding and the compassion that often issues forth from it that is your greatest tool in connecting with the client. Understanding allows you to be with the client. And being with the client is what the client will feel and how he will notice that you and he are connected.

Though generating connection is primarily your task as a coach, the client can participate in creating connection by being his authentic self, engaging fully in the session, and being honest about he wants most from life. In this way, the paths and bonds that are created are solid and true.

Related Terms/Phrases:
Align With
Ally With
Join
Partner

First Appearance: Fourth sentence in the eleventh paragraph of Contemplation Letter 5. Contemplation Letter 5 opens with, "It's good to see you…." The eleventh paragraph begins, "Because the profession is not regulated…." The fourth sentence starts, "There is also the opportunity…." (p. 14)

## Conscious

Definition – The part of the mind that exists inside of a person's awareness.

Further Thoughts: In Life Coaching, expansion of awareness and, therefore, a client's conscious mind is part of the process. The term, conscious mind, comes from Freud who first made the distinction between the information and mental processes in a person's awareness and those without. The opposite of the conscious mind is the unconscious mind.

Your role as the coach is to help a client access the thoughts and ideas in her unconscious mind. Unlike with therapy, you will not go rooting around in her thoughts via clinical methods. Rather, you will help create opportunities for the client to get know herself, especially through the identification of her wants and values. You will also help her access what she does know by taking the time to examine her experiences, especially her successes.

The role of the client is to be open to the process of learning about herself. As such, she will learn just how much she thinks and knows, about herself, others, and the world, even if that information is far from her every day thoughts. Over time, she will develop methods to increase the speed with which she can bring information from her mental depths to the surface.

Related Terms/Phrases:
Awareness
Conscious Mind

First Appearance: Fifth sentence in the eighth paragraph of Contemplation Letter 2. Contemplation Letter 2 opens with, ""Your mind may be filled with…." The eighth paragraph begins, "Are you ready to delve…." The fifth sentence starts, "To deeply explore…." (p. 7)

## Consulting

Definition – A profession that involves giving professional advice, solving problems, and providing other related services

Further Thoughts: In Life Coaching, advice is not given. Rather the client is taught ways to enhance his own thinking so he can come up with his own solutions. This is one of the primary distinctions between coaching and consulting.

Your role as the coach is to facilitate the client's thinking and not to do the thinking for him. Thus, your goal will be to stay away from consulting and to remain firmly grounded in coaching principles and approaches.

The client's role is to become comfortable with searching for his own answers. Over time, he will learn to ask for answers less and less and explore his own thoughts, feelings, perspectives, and possible solutions more and more.

Related Terms/Phrases:
Consultant
Consultation

First Appearance: First sentence in the eleventh paragraph of Contemplation Letter 2. Contemplation Letter 2 opens with, "Your mind may be filled with thoughts…." The eleventh paragraph begins, "If consulting is what calls to you…." The first sentence is the beginning of the eleventh paragraph and thus has the same start as the paragraph itself. (p. 7)

## Contribution

Definition – Something given or supplied

Further Thoughts: In Life Coaching, the client often finds that making a contribution to others or to the world is part of or is one of her purposes. This can come in the form of creating a product others can use, supplying others with a service they can benefit from, or donating her time or talent in some way.

Your role as the coach is to help the client determine what she would like to contribute and how she would like to make this contribution in the event that contribution seems of interest to her. Often, the notion comes up as part of values work. Thus, making sure to do values work in order to allow for the emergence of contribution as a value or purpose or part of a value or purpose is key. Supporting the client in her journey to making a contribution summarizes the remainder of your responsibility.

The client's role in addressing contribution is to share what she would like to give to others or the world. Then, she must explore how to make this contribution and stay committed to her path.

Again, contribution takes so many forms that it is likely that making a contribution will be part of the coaching dialogue in some way or other. If it is not, that is okay, too. The client drives the process not the coach or general patterns.

Related Terms/Phrases:
Addition
Donation
Gift
Legacy
Service

First Appearance: In plural form. Third sentence in the twenty-first paragraph of the Renewal Letter. The Renewal Letter opens with, "Having a Life Coaching business...." The twenty-first paragraph begins, "Maybe you are about to add a completely...." The third sentence starts, "To add to your list...." (p. 44)

## Core

Definition – The center or essence of a person, place, thing, or idea

Further Thoughts: In Life Coaching, core work is a large part of the work that is done. Put simply, working to define and build upon what makes the client the client is key. Understanding his values, which can also be thought of as his foundations as a person, is important.

Your role as the coach is to actively listen, ask thought-provoking questions, help create accountability measures, and assist in designing action plans. In this way, the most important seeds of the client's thought, feeling, and behavior patterns can be understood and used to further the achievement of his goals and dreams.

The client's role is to be willing to get to know his true self. He may come to coaching with a solid understanding of himself as a person or he may be quite unacquainted with who he is. In either case, there is always more to learn.

Related Terms/Phrases:
Essence
Self
Spirit

First Appearance: Second sentence in the sixth paragraph in Contribution Letter 3. Contribution Letter 3 opens with, "At this stage, you may be…." The sixth paragraph begins, "Every Life Coaching conversation includes…." The second sentence starts, "Appreciation is truly…." (p. 9)

## Core Belief

Definition – A fundamental assumption, often about oneself, others, the world, or life in general

Further Thoughts: In Life Coaching, core beliefs are discovered and uncovered through exploration of the client's basic thoughts and through contact with stumbling blocks that interrupt the client's movement toward her dreams. Frequently, stumbling blocks come in the form of limiting core beliefs that convince a client she can't when, in fact, she can.

Your role as the coach is to help the client learn about the beliefs that shape her life the most, whether by providing the hope and energy that push her toward her greatest accomplishments or by creating the doubt and dips in self-confidence that slow her progress toward her dreams. You can do this be reinforcing her positive attitudes toward herself and her abilities and by exploring and challenging what she sees as her limitations.

Core beliefs are often forged in a client's early years and are primarily discovered through the emergence of common themes. For instance, if a client continually thinks she cannot progress in any area that is dependent upon math, you might point out this pattern of lack of belief in herself. Through discussion, she might realize that she is not confident in her ability to work with numbers because she was always told, "Girls aren't good at math," a sentiment she eventually came to believe.

The client's role in uncovering and working with core beliefs is to be mindful of commonalities in her thoughts, especially those that tell her she can or cannot do something, as these tend to be related to core beliefs. She must also be willing to challenge those ideas that limit her

Related Terms/Phrases:
Core Assumption
Core Tenet
Life Theory
Self-View
Worldview

First Appearance: Sixth sentence in the eighteenth paragraph of the Renewal Letter. The Renewal Letter opens with, "Having a Life Coaching business…." The eighteenth paragraph begins, "Maybe you want to write…." The sixth sentence starts, "To present a method…." (p. 43)

## Disclosure

Definition – Information that is shared

Further Thoughts: In Life Coaching, disclosure occurs in every session. Throughout the process, the client is in charge of what he chooses to share. Though a client must be committed and have follow through to benefit from coaching, he is not required to share everything about himself. This gives him significant discretion in sharing his thoughts and feelings. The client frequently knows what is important to speak with you about and what is not necessarily relevant to coaching.

Your role as the coach is to support pertinent disclosure. On the rare occasion that the client is withholding key information, such as about lack of follow through with homework, you must let the client know you are aware of the withholding. You cannot demand that he disclose, but you can explain how the process is negatively impacted when pertinent information is not shared.

Related Terms/Phrases:
Admission
Answer
Shared Information

First Appearance: Sixth sentence in the fifth paragraph of Action Letter 6. Action Letter 6 opens with, "By now, you have set a few goals...." The fifth paragraph begins, "Have you already identified people...." The sixth sentence starts, "The finer points of confidentiality...." (p. 34)

## Doing

Definition – To bring to pass

Further Thoughts: In Life Coaching, doing is a regular process you and the client will engage in. At the start of the coaching relationship, the client is learning the steps to take to achieve success. There is a heavy focus on the means and ways goals can be accomplished, also known as the hows of coaching. Later, as the client becomes more comfortable with coaching and her new skills become habits, she will naturally do the things that benefit her. It is at this point that doing becomes being, which is the ultimate goal of coaching. When the client is successful at being her best self, she can be said to be successful at life.

You as the coach will also start with doing. At first, your primary guide to good coaching is doing the things you need to do to make the process a beneficial one for the client. You will begin by acclimatizing the client to the process, using legal and ethical guidelines to make coaching decisions, relying on your knowledge of strategies to address the issues at hand, etc. Later, with practice, coaching will flow more naturally from you. You will not have to think so hard. You will be available to follow your intuition. In fact, the longer you work in the field and the more comfortable you become with coaching, the more being is present in your work and the less you need to focus on doing.

Related Terms/Phrases:
Accomplishing
Achieving
Acting On
Carrying Out
Executing
Following Through
Implementing

First Appearance: First sentence in the eleventh paragraph of Action Letter 4. Action Letter 4 opens with, "You are graduating from training...." The eleventh paragraph begins, "Transitioning form learning to doing...." The first sentence is the beginning of the eleventh paragraph and thus has the same start as the paragraph itself. (p. 30)

## Dream

Definition – A vision or description of what the client wants in the future

Further Thoughts: In Life Coaching, dreams are the essence of the client's wants. Tied to those dreams are the values and whys, which give meaning to the client's aspirations. You and the client are both responsible for uncovering what the client most desires.

The client's role is to be open and honest in sharing his thoughts so, over time, what he most craves can be identified and turned into a goal or set of goals.

Your role as the coach is to listen to what the client is saying as well as what he isn't saying so you can help him learn to hear himself more clearly. Through this process of clarification, the client can better be understood and you and the client can design ways to help him thrive. By challenging the client and holding him accountable, you are assisting him in turning his dreams into a reality.

Related Terms/Phrases:
Aspiration
Desire
Hope
Vision
Wish

First Appearance: Second sentence in the first paragraph of Contemplation Letter 3. Contemplation Letter 3 opens with, "At this stage, you may be...." The first paragraph is the beginning of the letter and thus has the same beginning as the letter itself. The second sentence starts, "The answer: anyone with...." (p. 9)

## Effort

Definition – An exertion of force; attempt

Further Thoughts: In Life Coaching, effort is a significant focus of acknowledgement, appreciation, and celebration. Namely, the coaching process recognizes that the most the client has in any given situation is influence; control is not possible. Thus, rather then focus solely on results, you and the client must focus on the client's efforts.

The client's role is to try, not in name but in action. This means that as long as the client puts forth her best effort, she will be recognized for doing so. When she puts forth her less-than-best effort, you and she will explore the reasons and come up with a plan that allows her to apply her full self and abilities in the future.

Your role as the coach is to help the client see the importance of effort. You must also help the client learn to appreciate and acknowledge her effort so that she is more motivated and inspired to try things in the future, especially new things or things that are challenging. By being appreciative of effort, the client helps encourage herself to become more engaged with the process of living and her journey, rather than being hyperfocused on her destination.

Related Terms/Phrases:
Attempt
Endeavor
Try

First Appearance: In plural form. Third sentence in the third paragraph of the Pre-Contemplation Letter. The Pre-Contemplation Letter opens with, "You might be wondering why…." The third paragraph begins, "So, treasure yourself for making it…." The third sentence starts, "What do you think of when…." (p. 4)

## Empower

Definition – To promote the influence, effectiveness, or self-actualization of

Further Thoughts: In Life Coaching, the client is empowered throughout the process. One of the first steps in the client's empowerment is having someone listen. One of the most confidence boosting things the client can experience is being heard. Add to that your role in recognizing the brilliance in the client's thoughts, the legitimacy of the client's feelings, and the abilities the client possesses and the sky becomes the limit.

Your role as the coach is to be supportive, to encourage the client to become the best version of himself, to feel proud of who he is and what he is capable of accomplishing. The four primary pillars of coaching – listening, asking powerful questions, creating accountability, and design action plans – are your primary tools.

The client's role in becoming empowered is to be willing to better learn and appreciate himself. In order to do so, he must make himself vulnerable through the disclosure of his wants and dreams as well as the reasons behind them. This leap of faith is empowering in itself as it tells the client that not only can he survive being vulnerable, but he can benefit and grow from it.

Related Terms/Phrases:
Awaken
Build Up
Encourage
Legitimize

First Appearance: Third sentence in the nineteenth paragraph of the Renewal Letter. The Renewal Letter opens with, "Having a Life Coaching business...." The nineteenth paragraph begins, "Or maybe you would like...." The third sentence starts, "To demonstrate the form and use...." (p. 43)

# End

Definition – The portion of the Life Coaching session where discussion is brought to a close and accountability is agreed upon; also, the final leg of the Life Coaching relationship

Further Thoughts: In Life Coaching, the end of a session wraps up the day's agenda and sets the stage for the next appointment. During the end of the session, the client frequently decides upon homework and may even provide information about what she would like to talk about the next time.

You as the coach may be called upon to help flesh out the specifics of the client's accountability plan. You will often accomplish this by intensively listening to the client's ideas and reflecting on the feasibility of proposed steps and timelines. At times, it may behoove the client for you to make a few suggestions of your own. This can be helpful and keep the client in the driver's seat if you make sure that the client knows your thoughts are only options; they do not require agreement. This can also be helpful if you pose your suggestions as further food for thought, inviting the client to build upon and/or tailor them. Though, as with the other stages of the Life Coaching session, you will be called upon to function as a support, it is ultimately the client's responsibility to commit to what is to be done between sessions.

In order to further maximize productivity and benefit, during the end of the session, you may wish to have the client reflect upon her major takeaways from the session as well as identify what she did well throughout the process. With such an approach, the end of the session can aid the client in exiting the Thinking Space and re-entering the world with tools to enhance goal attainment and dream realization.

Related Terms/Phrases:
Close
Conclusion
Termination

First Appearance: Fourth sentence in the ninth paragraph of Action Letter 4. Action Letter 4 opens with, "You are graduating from training...." The ninth paragraph begins, "Would a visualization...." The fourth sentence starts, "Can you imagine what your ideal...." (p. 30)

**Energy**

Definition – A reserve of figurative or literal fuel that can be tapped into to create, attain, or understand

Further Thoughts: In Life Coaching, energy takes many forms. Common forms of energy include intellectual, emotional, physical, relational, and spiritual. You and the client are both responsible for bringing energy into the coaching session.

As the coach, you must do your best to either match the client's energy or use your energy to support the client in his thinking. The client is then tasked with accessing his intellectual and emotional energy to fuel his progress and create the life he wants to live. He must use his energy within and outside of the session to achieve his goals and reach his dreams.

Due to the support the client receives and the enthusiasm the coach has for his chosen path, the client will often find that his energy grows across the process and his ability to sustain energy is also increased. In addition, his motivation increases. This increase in motivation is an important benefit of coaching as many clients cite difficulties with motivation as one of the reasons they seek the support of a coach.

Related Terms/Phrases:
Fuel
Power
Spirit
Stamina
Strength
Vigor

First Appearance: Second sentence in the ninth paragraph of Action Letter 2. Action Letter 2 opens with, "Now that you have decided…." The ninth paragraph begins, "And other resources…." The second sentence is, "Such as energy?" (p. 26)

## Ethics

Definition – The moral principles that govern a profession

Further Thoughts: In Life Coaching, the coach is bound by guidelines – those set forth by the ethical principles of the field and those described in the laws and rules. At present, the International Coach federation (ICF) is the governing body that has tasked itself with the creation and maintenance of ethical principles for coaching.

Your role as the coach is to be familiar with and commit yourself to upholding both the laws and rules as well as the ethical principles of the field. When the two come into conflict, it is your job to forge a path of agreement between them when at all possible. Any questions you have can be directed to a mentor coach or a lawyer or both. In the event that a resolution cannot be reached, the law must be upheld.

The client's role in ethics is to be made aware of the basic tenets that affect her directly, such as discussion of the limits of confidentiality. The client, though not charged with upholding ethics, will benefit from your commitment to staying in line with the moral morays that guide the coaching relationship and process.

Related Terms/Phrases:
Code of Conduct
Ethical Standards
Morals

First Appearance: Third sentence in the third paragraph of Contemplation Letter 6. Contemplation Letter 6 opens with, "You may be wondering, 'How many choices....'" The third paragraph begins, "Of course, as is true with all decisions...." The third sentence starts, "They have made themselves responsible...." (p. 15)

## Factor

Definition – A person, place, thing, action, or process that contributes to an outcome or result

Further Thoughts: In Life Coaching, factors are often explored. The most important factors are those that either enhance or inhibit goal achievement. Contributing factors are factors that either help bring something into being or that help it to continue to exist. There are two main types of contributing factors: causal and maintenance. Causal factors are factors that increase or ensure the chance of something happening. Maintenance factors are factors that contribute to keeping things going.

On the other hand, there are also impeding factors, which are those that decrease or prevent the occurrence of something. There are two types of impeding factors: prohibitory and inhibitory. Prohibitory factors are those that prevent something from happening. Inhibitory factors are factors that decrease the chance of something happening, slow down its progress, or undermine its effectiveness.

Your role as the coach is to help identify factors that both enhance and impede the client's progress. Then, plans can be made to use those that help and work around or eliminate those that don't.

The client's role in identifying factors is to more closely look at successes and difficulties so that they can be uncovered and addressed. This is something he will do throughout the process.

Related Terms/Phrases:
Cause
Reason
Root
Source

First Appearance: In plural form. Fifth sentence in the third paragraph of Action Letter 8. Action Letter 8 opens with, "How are things going?" The third paragraph begins, "Did your adjustments primarily have...." The fifth sentence starts, "Did life factors drive you...." (p. 38)

## Failure

Definition – A lack of success or instance of falling short

Further Thoughts: In Life Coaching, failures technically do not exist. Instead, coming up short is seen as an opportunity to learn and grow. The client's role in addressing failure is to be honest about the times she is not able to achieve that she which she strove to achieve. She must also be willing to review what happened, including trying to identify the hiccups along the way.

Your role as the coach is first and foremost to help the client reframe failures so that they are not seen as impediments, but launching points for future success. Then, you are tasked with supporting the client through the disclosure of individual instances of coming up short as well as the exploration of such instances. Finally, you must help the client troubleshoot issues identified and create future plans so that any sought after success can be achieved with additional effort and an adapted approach.

Related Terms/Phrases:
Learning Opportunity
Opportunity for Growth
Teaching Moment

First Appearance: Fourth sentence in the tenth paragraph of Action Letter 7. Action Letter 7 opens with, "I hear you have started...." The tenth paragraph begins, "There are so many aspects...." The fourth sentence starts, "And often the fear of failure...." (p. 36)

## Feedback

Definition – An evaluation of or correction to information shared

Further Thoughts: In Life Coaching, the feedback provided is often positive in nature. Feedback that is not explicitly positive often comes in the form of a challenge. The client remains responsible for his choices and is, therefore, not given advice or guided down a particular path.

As a coach, your role in providing feedback is multi-faceted. You must first take in any and all pertinent information. This happens when you listen closely to what is being shared, pay attention to what is not being said, and observe with clarity the client's nonverbal cues. Once you can be certain you have heard the message, you can reflect back what has been shared and help the client see the connections between his disclosure and his identified objectives and goals. As part of your feedback, you will recognize and verbalize appreciation for what the client has already accomplished while also supporting him in his growth and movement forward toward his dreams.

The client's role is to share his true thoughts, feelings, and wishes throughout the process as well as to remain open to your reflection on how such thoughts, feelings, and wishes tie into his identified reason for seeking coaching. The client must then spend time strategizing how to use what he has learned from the feedback given to improve his life and pursue his dreams.

Related Terms/Phrases:
Critique
Evaluation
Food for Thought
Observation
Reflection

First Appearance: First sentence in the sixth paragraph of Contemplation Letter 3. Contemplation Letter 3 opens with, "At this stage, you may be wondering...." The sixth paragraph begins, "Every Life Coaching conversation includes...." The first sentence is the beginning of the sixth paragraph and thus has the same start as the paragraph itself. (p. 9)

## Feeling

Definition – An emotion or sentiment

Further Thoughts: In Life Coaching, feelings are understood and explored in connection to a client's thoughts. Feelings are a form of information and a part of the wisdom the client holds. The client's role is to share the feelings she has about her life situation and progress towards her goals. The type and number of feelings shared are up to her.

Your role as the coach is to use the information provided by the client's feelings to help her achieve her goals. Your purpose is not to delve into the client's emotional processes or past. You are simply letting what can be observed and confided inform you and the process so that the client can better understand herself and her wants. All work done with emotions is meant to guide the client toward her future.

Related Terms/Phrases:
Emotion
Sentiment

First Appearance: Fifth sentence in the third paragraph of the Pre-Contemplation Letter. The Pre-Contemplation letter opens with, "You might be wondering why…." The third paragraph begins, "So, treasure yourself…." The fifth sentence starts, "What feeling does that…." (p. 4)

## Fee Schedule

Definition – A menu of prices, often arranged by type and length of service

Further Thoughts: In Life Coaching, you are responsible for creating your fee schedule and explaining it to the client. It is best to go over your fee schedule prior to the first session.

Two primary approaches to fee schedules in coaching are the creation of fee-for-service pricing and the use of retainers for service. With fee-for-service pricing, the client pays a designated amount for a specific service. You have the choice between requiring the client to pay for the service prior to its occurrence or after. Most coaches require clients to pay for services prior to their occurrence, even if the payment is only a few minutes before the session.

When retainers are used, clients must purchase access to your services for a specific period of time. Typically, retainers last for a month or more. The amount paid is good for a select number and type of services during the designated period. Once that period of time has lapsed, a new retainer must be paid for further access to you as a coach. Typically, services not used during a previous month or set of months do not carry over though how to handle such unused services is up to you as the coach.

A hybrid of fee-for-service pricing and a retainer is the required package where the client must purchase a certain number of sessions up front. Often the time frame for the client to use such sessions is longer than with a retainer. Commonly, packages expire in a year.

The client's role in the implementation of the fee schedule is to understand and abide by it. If the client does not understand how payment works, then he is responsible for asking questions to clarify his confusion. If he wishes to ask for an exception to a rule, it is his responsibility to approach you with his request.

Related Terms/Phrases:
Charge
Fee
Service Menu
Services Offered

First Appearance: Fifth sentence in the tenth paragraph of Action Letter 6. Action Letter 6 opens with, "By now, you have set a few goals...." The tenth paragraph begins, "What are you seeking to make...." The fifth sentence is, "Created a fee schedule?" (p. 35)

## Flow

Definition – Fluidity; a state of optimal experience

Further Thoughts: In Life Coaching, the word flow is often used in two ways. As the coach, you may ask the client about how a process flowed. When asking this, you are asking about the process's ease and fluidity. When a process has a good flow along with positive results, it is thought to be effective and easy to implement or use.

You may also, if you choose, teach the client about the concept of an optimal experience. An optimal experience is one in which the client is highly engaged in what she is doing and very effective within the process. During a flow experience, the client often loses track of time and space. She may not even remember much about her experience as to her it will often feel like time has flown by.

The client's responsibility in regard to flow is to report to you how easy a process or strategy is to implement or use. In the event optimal experience has been covered and is being targeted, the client is also responsible for recognizing moments of flow and discussing them with you so that more flow experiences can be worked toward and achieved. The experience of a flow state is one that is often helpful to explore so that factors can be recreated when determined to be helpful in jumpstarting and promoting flow.

Related Terms/Phrases:
Ease
Optimal Experience
Progression

First Appearance: Third sentence in the second paragraph of Action Letter 7. Action Letter 7 opens with, "I hear you have started...." The second paragraph begins, "Have you had the chance...." The third sentence is, "To find your flow?" (p. 36)

## Future

Definition – A period in time that has yet to be

Further Thoughts: In Life Coaching, the future is the focus. The client comes to coaching in order to create the future he dreams of. You as the coach must help the client build his future through supportive listening and the creation and maintenance of progressive action.

The client's role is to be open to sharing his wishes and understanding what he truly wants to come to pass. Your role is to help the client prioritize what is most important and meaningful to him. Since the focus of Life Coaching is the future, all tools and strategies used are implemented for the purpose of creating the client's ideal future.

Related Terms/Phrases:
Days Ahead
Down the Road
Tomorrow

First Appearance: Seventh sentence in the sixth paragraph of Contemplation Letter 1. Contemplation Letter 1 opens with, "Your journey to becoming a Life Coach…." The sixth paragraph begins, "Why has your mind suggested…." The seventh sentence starts, "Or is the why a vision…." (p. 5)

## Gap

Definition – The space between what a client seeks and what the client has

Further Thoughts: In Life Coaching, the majority of the work you and the client do centers on closing the gap. This means you will both spend a great deal of your time in the gap, defining what it is and exploring its parameters. Then, through the coaching conversation, together you will devise and build a bridge between the two spheres. Accomplishment by accomplishment, the client will finally be equipped to turn possibility into being and successfully cross the divide between what is wanted to what is.

The client's role in this process is to share what she truly desires and what she presently has, especially as it relates to that which she seeks. This involves exploring thoughts and paying attention to feelings so that ought tos and shoulds are discarded, leaving only wants to take their place. Once the client knows where she is going, she can work with you to bring to fruition that which she has longed for.

Your role as the coach is to help the client explore and prioritize her wishes so that her dreams are no longer ephemeral wisps of imagination, but concrete goals she can set and reach. In working alongside the client within the gap, you are tasked with believing that the client wants what she says she wants as well as supporting her in her pursuits.

Related Terms/Phrases:
Chasm
Difference Between
Disparity
Discrepancy
Incongruity Between

First Appearance: Eighth sentence in the sixth paragraph of Action Letter 3. Action Letter 3 opens with, "I imagine your mind is...." The sixth paragraph begins, "You might not think...." The eighth sentence starts, "Or sad if you are having difficulty...." (p. 28)

## Goal

Definition – Objective

Further Thoughts: In Life Coaching, goals are created from the client's dreams, wants, and wishes. Goals consist of concrete steps meant to take the client from where he is to where he wants to go. Goals are often thought of as small and short-term or large and long-term. Short-term goals are frequently assigned time frames for completion that vary from a day to a week to a month. Long-term goals tend to require multiple months, a year, or multiple years to complete.

The client's role in goal creation and setting is to be honest and open with his thoughts and feelings so that what he desires can rise to the forefront of his mind and be planned for.

Your role as the coach is to support the client in creating goals that are specific and achievable. In order to do this, you must take into account what you know about the client and how he works. By helping him see where his strengths lie, how he has best achieved success in the past, and where he can focus his attention to make improvements, you can not only exponentially increase his probability of success but you can also shorten the time frame in which he achieves it.

If you wish you may adapt the use of S.M.A.R.T. goals where S stands for Specific, M for Measurable, A for Attainable, R for Realistic, and T for Timely. The aim of S.M.A.R.T. goals is to define goals enough that it is clear how and when they are achieved.

Related Terms/Phrases:
Action
How To
Marker

Means
Step
What

First Appearance: Second sentence in the ninth paragraph of Contemplation Letter 4. Contemplation Letter 4 opens with, "It's at this stage...." The ninth paragraph begins, "As can be seen...." The second sentence starts, "Whatever the name, wherever the service...." (p. 11)

## Gratitude

Definition – The state of being appreciative or thankful

Further Thoughts: In Life Coaching, happiness is one of the client's primary goals. And those professionals who study happiness have found that gratitude is its key component. Being grateful for what one has promotes satisfaction with life; satisfaction with life, in turn, enhances the client's ability to experience joy.

Your role as the coach is to help educate the client on the role of gratitude in happiness and the nature of happiness, including the amount of happiness a person can expect to have. In terms of how the client will experience happiness, it is important that she understand that not every moment in life will be a happy one. Still, even with this natural limitation, it is possible for her to lead an overall happy life.

The client's role in gratitude is to make a commitment to taking time to appreciate who she is, what she has, and what she has accomplished. One method she can use to check in with gratitude and to access her appreciation over time is through the use of a gratitude journal. Typically, when keeping a gratitude journal, the client writes two things she is thankful for each day. She is then free to decide how often she will look over what she has already written. This perusal of appreciation can be used to sustain positive momentum or to jumpstart future projects and dreams. It is up to the client.

Related Terms/Phrases:
Acknowledgement
Appreciation
Recognition
Thankfulness

First Appearance: Second sentence in the fourth paragraph of the Legacy Letter. The Legacy Letter opens with, "We meet at...." The fourth paragraph begins, "You have introduced the importance...." The second sentence starts, "They understand the significance...." (p. 47)

## Habit

Definition – A tendency or pattern, often of behavior

Further Thoughts: In Life Coaching, the client often comes to services in order to create good habits and relinquish bad ones. In some cases, it may be hard for him to distinguish between what is helpful and what is not. In other cases, when he does know, it may be hard for him to leave certain tendencies behind.

Your role as the coach is to note the presence of habits and help the client explore the impact of such behavioral patterns on his progress toward dreams and goals. In the case of unwanted or unhelpful habits, it is your job to help the client create a path to change and then to support his efforts along that path. When it is necessary for you to help the client create a good habit, again you must help in the planning phase when required and support his execution of the plan.

The client's role is to be open to recognizing patterns and to making changes to those that are not helpful or that impede positive growth and development. Though habits are most often referenced in terms of behaviors, it is possible for the client to develop thought and feeling habits, which can often benefit from exploration. The goal, of course, is only for the client to understand enough about his tendencies to be able to move toward that which he wants to achieve.

If a significantly unhealthy or life-threatening habit is disclosed such as alcohol or drug abuse, it is your job to make a referral to a mental health professional. In such a case, it would also be wise to tell the client to inform his primary care physician as well.

Related Terms/Phrases:
Pattern
Ritual
Tendency

First Appearance: In plural form. Third sentence in the third paragraph of the Legacy Letter. The Legacy Letter opens with, "We meet at...." The third paragraph begins, "You have helped people...." The third sentence starts, "Helping them source...." (p. 47)

## Homework

Definition – An experience to be had or an assignment to be completed by the client between sessions

Further Thoughts: In Life Coaching, homework is an important part of the process. The majority of life is lived outside of the coaching session. Therefore, it is important to establish that the majority of work will be done outside of the coaching session. Homework is one part of this.

Your role as the coach is to help the client create homework assignments that are meaningful and that move her toward the achievement of her goals. In Life Coaching, there is no room for busy work. Assignments given must have purpose. You must as the coach also check in with how homework went. Success can then be recognized and celebrated while difficulties can be troubleshot so a new approach can be formulated.

The client's role is to remain engaged with the purpose and meaning of the coaching process outside of the session through the completion of homework assignments and the implementation of techniques learned in coaching. The client is also a significant part of the homework creation process. Finally, the client has the final say in deciding upon what to do for homework.

Related Terms/Phrases:
Assignment
Experience
Experiment
Task

First Appearance: Third sentence in the eighteenth paragraph of the Renewal Letter. The Renewal Letter opens with, "Having a Life Coaching business...." The eighteenth paragraph begins, "Maybe you want to write...." The third sentence starts, "To teach the upcoming generation...." (p. 43)

## How

Definition – By what path or to what degree

Further Thoughts: In Life Coaching, hows are an essential portion of the meat of the process. They help delineate the manner in which a client will achieve his goals as well as the length of time it will take for him to achieve them. Hows are the bulk of action plans and accountability measures.

The role of the client is to share the ideas he has for achieving his goals, including any previous attempts he has made. He must also stay engaged in the exploration of what has been tried and be open to feedback related to what went well and what didn't. In this way, the client can, by the end, create an individualized plan that capitalizes on his abilities and past experience.

Your role as the coach is to support the client during this process. You must listen and ask questions that help the client to create his own answers and methods. By doing this, you will help the client to devise hows that are both measurable and achievable. In this way, you are ensuring that the effort the client puts forth bears him fruit.

Related Terms/Phrases:
Approach
Goal
Means
Method
Plan
Script

First Appearance: In plural form. Third sentence in the fourth paragraph of Contemplation Letter 1. Contemplation Letter 1 opens with, "Your journey to becoming a Life Coach began…." The fourth paragraph begins, "There are many questions you can ask…" The third sentence in the paragraph is, "Others with hows." (p. 5)

## Humor

Definition – A sense of what is funny

Further Thoughts: In Life Coaching, humor is not only allowed, it is suggested. Of course, it is important to establish that the client is open to play, including the use of humor, prior to engaging in its expression in session.

Your role as the coach is to appreciate the client's use of humor and to introduce appropriate humor of your own when it is of benefit to the client. The client's role in the use of humor is to use it if she so wishes.

It is not necessary for you and the client to become riotous in session, only to allow humor to work on you in a positive way. Humor is often helpful when the client is feeling frustrated and would like to discharge some of that frustration in a healthy way or see a stumbling block or inhibitory factor in a different light. Humor also helps discharge the tension associated with nerves.

Related Terms/Phrases:
Funny
Joke
Jovial
Mirth

First Appearance: Fourth sentence in the eighteenth paragraph of the Renewal Letter. The Renewal Letter opens with, "Having a Life Coaching business…." The eighteenth paragraph begins, "Maybe you want to write…." The fourth sentence starts, "To illustrate the use of…." (p. 43)

## Ideal

Definition – Perfect example, idea, or vision

Further Thoughts: In Life Coaching, ideals are aspirations. That is to say, you as the coach know perfection is not possible and part of your job in working with ideals is to make sure the client knows this as well.

As the coach, you can help the client envision a dream, which is often an ideal, and work toward that dream, knowing that the client's existence in the realm of flesh, blood, and reality will require some accommodation of the dream to the rules of life on Earth. Thus, as the dream starts to come true in various ways through the attainment of goals, it is helpful for the client to be grateful for what he has even if it doesn't look exactly like he first imagined.

The client's role is to understand the purpose of an ideal and to use that function to help him achieve what he wants as well as appreciate the form in which his wish arrives.

Related Terms/Phrases:
Aspiration
Perfect
Quintessential
Utmost

First Appearance: First sentence in the second paragraph of Action Letter 6. Action Letter 6 opens with, "By now, you have set a few goals...." The second paragraph begins, "Have you defined...." The first sentence is the beginning of the second paragraph and thus has the same start as the paragraph itself. (p. 34)

## Identity

Definition – A person's character or personality

Further Thoughts: In Life Coaching, the client's identity comes into play in many ways. First off, the client is often trying to make changes to her life, which involves closing the gap between who she wants to be and how she sees herself. Therefore, in some ways, the client is likely dissatisfied with her identity. In many cases, this dissatisfaction relates to a specific area of her life or a specific portion of an area of her life.

Your role as the coach is to help the client become the person she wants to be. In this way, you will be supporting her as she actively changes her identity, by either creating new facets of herself and her experience or further developing those she wishes to maximize.

The client's role is to take an honest accounting of her life and herself and to share with you that which she wants to change or enhance. This can be a time of great vulnerability for the client. Therefore, it is important that you help the client understand that she has many great qualities and that the changes she is making represent small tweaks that will have great reward because they will better align her life with what she most wants.

Related Terms/Phrases:
Self-Concept
Self-Perception

First Appearance: First sentence in the ninth paragraph of Contemplation Letter 3. Contemplation Letter 3 opens with, "At this stage, you may be wondering...." The ninth paragraph begins, "If the block is less substantial...." The first sentence is the beginning of the ninth paragraph and thus has the same start as the paragraph itself. (p. 10)

## Influence

Definition – The ability to create an effect or move toward a desired aim

Further Thoughts: In Life Coaching, influence is a word that is used in lieu of control. It is a myth that people can have complete control over themselves, others, or even their small corner of the world. However, that doesn't stop them from striving for such control and being upset when they come up short.

In order to start the coaching process off on the right foot, it is often helpful for you as the coach to introduce the idea of having influence versus having control. In this way, you are preparing the client for the emergence of inevitable challenges or roadblocks that he would not choose, but which he will be charged with navigating. Understanding there are limits in life and that those limits can be adapted to and addressed is key to the pursuit and attainment of happiness.

The client's role in terms of influence is to accept it as an honest alternative to the myth of control and to engage it when it is helpful and healthy to do so. By following his dreams, he is executing his influence upon his life. By using influence, he is working toward all that he dreams.

Related Terms/Phrases:
Have an Effect
Make a Difference

First Appearance: Fifth sentence in the eighteenth paragraph of the Renewal Letter. The Renewal Letter opens with, "Having a Life Coaching business...." The eighteenth paragraph begins, "Maybe you want to write...." The fifth sentence starts, "To explain how to teach...." (p. 43)

## Inspire

Definition – To animate or enliven, often toward a purpose

Further Thoughts: In Life Coaching, the client often hopes to be inspired as part of the process. The inspiration the client wants depends on her values and what matters most to her. Often, she craves inspiration not just to achieve her dreams, but also to live life to its fullest.

Your role as the coach is to help the client get in touch with the things that inspire her, whether they are things she comes into contact with on a regular basis or those she must seek out. In addition, you may also find yourself helping her to discover new things and experiences to inspire her so that she can cycle these inspirations in and out of her life, as she so chooses, and thereby leech them of their maximum benefit.

The client's role is to recognize that she craves inspiration and to find regular ways to include that which inspires her in her life. She is then charged with using this energy to pursue her goals and dreams so that her entire life becomes an unending source of inspiration for her.

Related Terms/Phrases:
Embolden
Excite
Galvanize
Hearten
Spark

First Appearance: In past tense. Second sentence in the tenth paragraph of Action Letter 1. Action Letter 1 opens with, "With each new addi-tion...." The tenth paragraph begins, "Or, as can also be common...." The second sentence starts, "Inspired you to do something...." (p. 24)

## Interest

Definition – Attention; appreciation; investment in

Further Thoughts: In Life Coaching, it is paramount that you show interest in the client and his thoughts, feelings, values, dreams, and wants. The primary ways you do this are by listening and asking powerful questions. By helping the client create accountability and design action plans, you are also displaying interest in the client, especially his goals and dreams, as well as demonstrating your intent to remain interested in him and his life.

The client's role in regard to interest is to develop and sustain investment in that which he wants most. Rather than just going through the motions, he is tasked with cultivating a keen appreciation for and engagement with the things that make him happy. In this way he is becoming interested in himself as a person and in the journey of his life. He is living not just existing. And choosing to live versus survive is one of the most active signs of interest there is.

Related Terms/Phrases:
Concern
Enthusiasm
Passion

First Appearance: Third sentence in the eighteenth paragraph of the Renewal Letter. The Renewal Letter opens with, "Having a Life Coaching business…." The eighteenth paragraph begins, "Maybe you want to write…." The third sentence starts, "To teach the upcoming generation…." (p. 43)

## Intuition

Definition – Insight; natural sense

Further Thoughts: In Life Coaching, intuition is developed and used by both you and the client. The more you work as a coach, the more you develop a natural instinct for when to listen, when to ask a powerful question, when to focus on accountability, when to work on designing an action plan, and when to just be in the moment.

Over time, you will feel rather than just think your way to the right approach at the right time. This will have you shifting between providing direct support to the client and leaving her room to practice supporting herself. Thus, your role as a coach in regard to intuition is to develop it through regular practice and then use it masterfully.

The client's role in terms of intuition is to develop and use her own. The client's intuition is aimed at improving her life and circumstances. By modeling your use and comfort with it is a coach, you will be teaching the client that listening to her inner voice is not only okay, but essential to a well-lived life. For some clients, a direct discussion about intuition is also helpful in its use and expansion. Exercises aimed at getting a client back in touch with her inner self and its instincts can be of assistance as well.

Related Terms/Phrases:
Inner Voice
Inner Wisdom
Insight
Natural Instinct

First Appearance: Third sentence in the twentieth paragraph of the Renewal Letter. The Renewal Letter opens with, "Having a Life Coaching business...." The twentieth paragraph begins, "Or maybe you want...." The third sentence starts, "So they can show their classes...." (p. 43)

## Invitation

Definition – A request for someone's presence or participation; also, a presented opportunity to think, feel, or behave in a certain way

Further Thoughts: In Life Coaching, identifying and responding to invitations for the purpose of furthering the client's agenda is a regular practice. Utilizing invitations in an effective and productive manner often starts with educating the client about the nature of invitations.

To start, you may be called upon to distinguish invitations from causes. Simply put, an invitation is a situation or factor that offers the client the opportunity to think, feel, or behave in a certain way if he so chooses. A cause creates a particular effect; choice is limited if present at all.

When the client understands what an invitation is, he can see that he is not a push button for others or the environment. He can understand he actively makes choices in how he will think, feel, and act on a daily basis. This allows him to seize opportunities for making different choices in situations where he previously felt stuck or controlled by the events around him. Increasing the client's sense of efficacy and personal responsibility is one of the primary functions of invitation identification.

Related Terms/Phrases:
Opportunity
Option
Request

First Appearance: Fifth sentence in the second paragraph of the Renewal Letter. The Renewal Letter opens with, "Having a Life Coaching business...." The second paragraph begins, "You are evolving...." The fifth sentence starts, "You might be craving a new...."
(p. 41)

## Journey

Definition – Path of travel; process of moving from one place to another

Further Thoughts: In Life Coaching, the focus is on assisting the client in appreciating and benefitting from the journey of her life. This focus is often in direct opposition to the modern approach to life, which typically values outcomes and destinations to effort and processes.

Your role as the coach is to help the client understand that appreciating and becoming comfortable with the journey of life is essential for ongoing and replicable happiness. The best the client will ever have is influence over her life. She cannot guarantee outcomes no matter how great her talent or abilities. Thus, acknowledging what she puts into her life and the fluid nature of moving from point A to point B is essential so that she can weather bumps in the road and ultimately use them as springboards for later success.

The client's role is to learn to appreciate the path she is on not just the attainment of goals. It is possible to be engaged in life every day; it is not possible to achieve a new dream, such as climbing to the summit of a mountain, every twenty-four hours. If the client can learn to be, her ability to experience joy and be satisfied with who she, what she has, and what she has done is exponentially increased.

Related Terms/Phrases:
Adventure
Course
Path
Pilgrimage
Process
Road
Sojourn

First Appearance: Third sentence in the third paragraph of the Introduction Letter. The Introduction Letter begins, "Somehow this book has found its way to you." The third paragraph begins, "What follows are a series of letters…." The third sentence starts, "For those recently started on the journey…." (p. 3)

# Joy

Definition – Happiness; a source of delight or enthusiasm for life

Further Thoughts: In Life Coaching, joy is the goal. Moments of joy. As a coach, you recognize that joy cannot be experienced every moment of every day. You also recognize that moments of joy, especially those that are in line with the client's values and most treasured wants, are the foundation for a happy life. Part of your role is to help the client understand that joy can be experienced but not hoarded.

Another part of your role as a coach is to help point out to the client the times when he is expressing joy with his words, facial expression, body language, or actions. It might seem that the client will always know when he is happy, but that is not always the case. Since human beings can feel more than one emotion at a time, it is possible for a seed of happiness to fail to be noticed or grown. The more he recognizes when he is experiencing joy, the better able he will be to understand its underpinnings and recreate it.

In fact, the client's role in creating and appreciating moments of joy is significant. Often, he has come to coaching in order to experience more joy. He may have to start by identifying that which brings him joy. Or he may already know. He may have to find ways to pursue that which he values most or he may only need help in maintaining his achievements over time. His role might involve doing more or doing less. Regardless, the experience of and appreciation of joy is an integral part of a well-lived life and, thus, an important part of coaching.

Related Terms/Phrases:
Bliss
Delight
Elation
Enthusiasm
Glee

Happiness
Satisfaction
Wonder

First Appearance: Fifth sentence in the eleventh paragraph of Action Letters 6. Action Letters 6 opens with, "By now, you have set a few goals...." The eleventh paragraph begins, "The questions that can be asked...." The fifth sentence starts, "Yet, for those who manage their time and energies...." (p. 35)

## Laws and Rules

Definition – State- or federal-issued guideline with an accompanying penalty for breach of adherence

Further Thoughts: In Life Coaching, laws, or laws and rules as they are often referred to, must be followed. Typically, laws that are most applicable to the running of a business are issued by the state though it is important to be aware of any federal laws with which you must stay in compliance.

You as the coach are responsible for being in line with the law. Ignorance is not an excuse. Thus, it is often helpful to consult with an attorney, especially when opening a business or making changes to an existing one, to make sure you that you are aware of all of your responsibilities.

At this time, Life Coaching is not a licensed profession, which means you are not required to obtain training, take a state test, or complete continuing education to be able to work as a Life Coach. Still, it is suggested that you receive some form of education in order to be effective and be able to support your clients well.

The client's role in laws and rules is to be made aware of any that she must be made aware of in the intake phase. One example is being told you will be keeping a record of your services, which in relationship to the law means your records serve as proof that sessions occurred. This relates to documenting that you were paid for a reason. If you keep your financial records separate from your coaching records, the client should be made aware of that as well.

Related Terms/Phrases:
Professional Guidelines

First Appearance: Third sentence in the third paragraph of Contemplation Letter 6. Contemplation Letter 6 opens with, "You may be wondering, 'How many choices....'" The third paragraph begins, "Of course, as is true with all decisions...." The third sentence starts, "They have made themselves responsible...." (p. 15)

## Learning History

Definition – A collection of beliefs and assumed truths developed over time, starting in childhood

Further Thoughts: In Life Coaching, the present and the future are the primary focus. On occasion, addressing the role of the past and its relationship to what the client is working on in the here and now will be of assistance. Understanding learning history is one of those occasions.

You as the coach can explain to the client that many of the lessons he learned, especially those that govern how he thinks he and others should behave and how the world works, were learned early in his life, likely in childhood. You can explain that many of these assumptions are faulty, the result of childhood logic. Knowing this can help the client identify limiting core beliefs and help him remove them as stumbling blocks. The goal is not to process the client's childhood but to provide minimal guidance in understanding where limiting beliefs come from and how to address them. Explaining that they are the result of childhood conclusions often helps move the client toward changing that which would benefit him to change.

The client's role in regard to learning history is to be open to making alterations to outdated, incorrect, and/or limiting core beliefs. His exploration of such beliefs will occur as a belief is encountered. Unhelpful beliefs will be addressed when they present as stumbling blocks standing in the way of his dreams.

Learning history can also contain positive, correct beliefs. Those, of course, are kept and often nurtured.

Related Terms/Phrases:
Childhood Lessons
Life Lessons
Life Perspective

First Appearance: First sentence in the fourth paragraph of Action Letter 2. Action Letter 2 opens with, "Now that you have decided...." The fourth paragraph begins, "It might be helpful to know...." The first sentence is the beginning of the fourth paragraph and thus has the same start as the paragraph itself. (p. 26)

## Life Coach

Definition – A professional who supports a client in working toward her goals and dreams by listening, asking powerful questions, creating accountability, and designing action plans

Further Thoughts: In Life Coaching, there is a basic formula for helping the client. This formula includes four pillars: listening, asking powerful questions, creating accountability, and designing action plans. Life Coaches uses these tools to help their clients. Therefore, you, as a coach, will be using these tools as well.

What varies between coaches are style and specialty. Namely, style is the manner in which these four pillars are approached. In many cases, style can be influenced by education. Some schools of coaching place a significant emphasis on having fun. Others are more about getting down to brass tacks and providing a deeply meaningful service. Specialty refers to the many areas of a client's life that can be worked on, such as self, relationships, career, spirituality, etc. Specialty can also be determined by the place where services are provided or to whom services are provided, such as in a corporate setting to executives.

The client's role in relationship to the Life Coach is to seek out and work with one that is a good fit and who specializes in what the client wants to work on. The client starts this process though it may have to later be guided by the coach if a referral is needed.

Related Terms/Phrases:
Coach

First Appearance: Third sentence in the third paragraph of the Intro-duction Letter. The Introduction Letter opens with, "Somehow this book has found its way…." The third paragraph begins, "What follows are a series of letters…." The third sentence starts, ""For those recently started on the journey…." (p. 3)

## Life Coaching

Definition – The process by which a Life Coach helps a client achieve his goals and work toward his dreams, which includes the acts of listening, asking powerful questions, creating accountability, and designing action plans

Further Thoughts: In Life Coaching, there is a formula for achieving success. At the center of the coaching formula are the four pillars of coaching: listening, asking powerful questions, creating accountability, and designing action plans. Every coach uses these skills to support the client's growth and achievement.

Life Coaching is often simply referred to as coaching in certain settings, such as the executive world. It can also be referred to by its area of specialty, such as Career Coaching, Relationship Coaching, Spiritual Coaching, etc. Each of these, in the end, is a form of Life Coaching.

Life Coaching involves you as the coach and the client working together in a collaborative process in order to create a Thinking Space and assist the client in achieving his goals and dreams. Your style of approach and the exact manner in which you help clients achieve success is up to you and is likely influenced by your training.

Related Terms/Phrases:
Coaching

First Appearance: First sentence in the third paragraph of the Introduction Letter. The Introduction Letter opens with, "Somehow this book has found its way…." The third paragraph begins, "What follows are a series of letters…." The first sentence is the beginning of the third paragraph and thus has the same start as the paragraph itself. (p. 3)

## Life Phase

Definition – Stage of life, often accompanied by a discernable set of wants or goals and influenced by societal expectations

Further Thoughts: In Life Coaching, the client comes to the process at a certain time in her life. Whether she is in her early 20s, preparing to start a career or a family, or in her late 90s, curious as to what her 100th year can bring her, she has a dream or a set of goals she would like to work towards. Sometimes, the dream or set of goals is specific. At other times, it is only a vague inkling of wanting something different or more.

A person's life phase comes into coaching as a factor that can be checked in with. For instance, the client in her early 20s is likely facing a lot of firsts and may want help navigating those. Plus, she may wish to map out her next several decades. The client in her late 90s may wish to find renewed passion as many of her firsts have long since been met and handled. She may want to create new experiences that differ from her old ones or she may wish to revisit those activities and experiences she treasured most during her life.

Part of your role as the coach is to understand the role that the client's developmental stage plays in her goal and dream creation. It may be helpful to check in with theories on the topic, such as Erik Erikson's Theory of Psychosocial Development or Abraham Maslow's Hierarchy of Needs. Of course, it is important to remember that expectations can vary across societies and generations.

The client's role in terms of life phase is to be willing to share what she wants in the present and to work toward making sure such wants are truly hers. Due to the nature of socialization, it is possible for the client to come in with a list of ought tos and shoulds that are masquerading as her wishes. Over time, a lack of enthusiasm for her dreams will reveal when and where these are present and allow the client to modify her list of goals until they are satisfying and rewarding to her.

Related Terms/Phrases:
Act of Life
Developmental Stage

First Appearance: Fourth sentence in the first paragraph of Contemplation Letter 1. Contemplation Letter 1 opens with, "Your journey to becoming a Life Coach...." The first paragraph is the beginning of the letter and thus has the same beginning as the letter itself. The fourth sentence starts, "It might have come to you as you were...." (p. 5)

## Life Wheel

Definition – A graph for helping a client rate his present satisfaction with various life areas as well as what level of satisfaction he would like to achieve for each one in the future

Further Thoughts: In Life Coaching, the life wheel is often used as an intake tool to help gauge where the client is in regard to satisfaction with various areas of his life. Commonly, the life wheel has eight pieces that are presented in a pie graph. Depending on the creator of the particular life wheel, which also goes by other names such as the coaching mandala, the names of these eight pieces vary. Typically, however, they include a version quite similar to the following: personal growth, career, significant other, fun and hobbies, spirituality, friends and family, finances, and health and wellness. If you choose to use a life wheel as part of your intake procedure or any part of your coaching process, you are welcome to have as many puzzle pieces as you like and name them what you wish.

The purpose of the life wheel is to have a client rate his satisfaction with the selected life areas, which results in a quick snapshot of where he is now. Then, this snapshot is contrasted with where he would like to be. Typically, the ratings are on a 0- to 10-point scale, where 0 means no satisfaction and 10 is the highest level of satisfaction imaginable. 5-point, 6-point, and 8-point scales are also common.

Though it might seem that every client will choose a ten for what he wishes to achieve in each life area, that is not always the case. And, of course, present ratings of satisfaction vary from person to person.

Your role as a coach in the use of the life wheel is to explain it and periodically check in with where the client is in any or all areas of focus. When the life wheel is used as part of coaching, it can serve as a measure of the process's effectiveness. The client's role is to be honest about present ratings and forthcoming about where he would like to end up.

Related Terms/Phrases:
Coaching Mandala

First Appearance: Sixth sentence in the twelfth paragraph of Action Letter 8. Action Letter 8 opens with, "How are things going?" The twelfth paragraph begins, "Are there platforms you wish…." The sixth sentence starts, "Or an animated comparative…." (p. 39)

## Listening

Definition – The act of hearing and paying attention to what a person is communicating

Further Thoughts: In Life Coaching, listening goes beyond just hearing. Listening, at its deepest level, includes processing the client's verbal and nonverbal cues so that the entirety of her message is taken in and understood.

Your role as the coach is to listen and listen well. Listening is an active process. It requires the engagement of your mind and intuition so that, when you reflect back and ask for further clarification, you are using both what you heard and what you didn't to communicate. At its best, listening can be a transformational process that assists the client in growing into the person she would like to become.

The role of the client is to share what is on her mind and participate in an interchange that helps her clarify her thoughts and feelings. Over time, she will get to know herself better and become acquainted with thoughts she didn't know she had.

The marker for collaboration in the listening process is your ability to listen with the client and the client's ability to listen with you. In this way, you are both partners in the communication process and the client's thinking is the center of what is to be explored and understood.

Related Terms/Phrases:
Active Listening
Auditorily Processing
Hearing
Transformational Listening

First Appearance: First sentence in the ninth paragraph of Contemplation Letter 1. Contemplation Letter 1 opens with, "Your journey to
becoming a Life Coach...." The ninth paragraph begins, "No matter
where the idea of Life Coaching...." The first sentence is the beginning
of the ninth paragraph and thus has the same start as the paragraph
itself. (p. 5)

## Mastery

Definition – The consistent ability to replicate a skill or engage in a process with acumen

Further Thoughts: In Life Coaching, mastery is the goal. Mastery is part of your horizon as a coach, what you are keeping in your sights and moving towards. Mastery is also part of the client's goal set, as he will wish to be able to engage with life in a consistent and meaningful way.

Your role in mastery is to educate yourself about the skills, tools, and strategies you will need to become a great Life Coach. Then, you must regularly use them so that you move from doing to being. When you are being a Life Coach, embodying all that the profession has to offer, you are working from mastery.

The client's role is to decide what is most important for him to master. In general, the client will wish to become a master at living his own life. But the skills he will need and the areas he will focus on will vary depending on his dreams and values.

Related Terms/Phrases:
Adroitness
Competence
Expertness
Grasp
Proficiency

First Appearance: Third sentence in the seventeenth paragraph of Contemplation Letter 6. Contemplation Letter 6 opens with, "You may be wondering, 'How many choices....'" The seventeenth paragraph begins, "The IAC indicates that this particular definition...." The third sentence starts, "That they are working toward...." (p. 17)

## Mentor

Definition – An overseer or guide

Further Thoughts: In Life Coaching, accreditation by any of the most preeminent governing bodies requires proof of mentorship hours. Having a mentor serves more of a purpose than qualifying for additional certifications, however.

If you as a coach work with a mentor, you are better able to hone your craft and advance your skills. Since you will be working with someone who has been where you are and who has come out the other side, you are in a special position to advance your understanding of not only the Life Coaching process but the trajectory of a Life Coaching career.

As with any other relationship, it is important to find a mentor who is a good fit for you. At the more advanced levels of mentoring, it is also important that your mentor have experience in the areas you would like to work in. This will allow you to get specific and credible feedback about your strengths and the areas in which you need to grow.

In truth, a mentor coach will fluctuate between true coaching and consulting. Coaching will occur when the focus is your thoughts. Consulting occurs when the mentor coach provides his or her view of what you are doing well and what you can improve. This move into consulting occurs most often during the review of your recorded sessions.

When you are the mentee, you are the client and therefore must be honest and forthcoming with your thoughts about and work in coaching. If you choose to become a mentor coach yourself, you must then apply all of your coaching skills to support the new or eager to learn coach along her journey.

Related Terms/Phrases:
Supervisor

First Appearance: Third sentence in the sixth paragraph of Action Letter 6. Action Letter 6 opens with, "By now, you have set a few goals…." The sixth paragraph begins, "Have you sought out Life Coaching…." The third sentence starts, "Do you have a mentor…." (p. 34)

## Metabehavior

Definition – The way you act in response to awareness of your actions

Further Thoughts: In Life Coaching, meta- is an important prefix. It refers to the response to an earlier phase of the same category of thought, feeling, action, or experience. Metabehavior refers specifically to those actions that result in response to awareness of other actions.

Your role as a coach is to help a client understand when metabehavior is occurring and what it means. For instance, the client might be honest and open about his general habits and tendencies. This is one behavioral approach to his general behaviors. Or he might deny that he behaves a certain way and try to act in opposite or opposing ways to conceal his general patterns. This is another behavioral approach to general behaviors. Changing habits is one of the most common forms of metabehavior as it is a response to the regular core actions in a person's life.

The client's role in regard to metabehavior is to engage in dialogue about his and make changes as appropriate. For the client, metabehavior may be an easy thing to discuss or a more difficult concept to grasp. If he has difficulty understanding or utilizing metabehavioral techniques, it is also his job to clarify what he doesn't understand by first asking questions.

Related Terms/Phrases:
Meta-action
Meta-choice
Meta-habit

First Appearance: Third sentence in the second paragraph of Action Letter 4. Action Letter 4 opens with, "You are graduating from training...." The second paragraph begins, "Are you still anxiously exploring...." The third sentence is, "Metabehavior?" (p. 30)

## Metacommunication

Definition – Conversation about a conversation or conversational pattern

Further Thoughts: In Life Coaching, metacommunication is a significant process. It is constantly being engaged in. In fact, metacommunication is likely present in some way or another during every coaching session.

Your role as the coach is to help the client better understand what her communication and communication patterns are telling her. In this way, metacommunication is used as a guide to improving both communication and living. An example of metacommunication is when you as the coach say something like, "You smiled when you said that" or "Your voice changes whenever we discuss this topic."

The client's role in terms of metacommunication is to be open to learning more about how she communicates and what that can teach her. For maximum benefit, she must move from hearing commentary and processing it to making observations and providing commentary of her own.

Related Terms/Phrases:
Metaconversation
Metadiscussion

First Appearance: Second sentence in the second paragraph of Action Letter 4. Action Letter 4 opens with, "You are graduating from training…." The second paragraph begins, "Are you still anxiously exploring…." The second sentence is, "Metacommunication?" (p. 30)

## Metafeeling

Definition – Emotion about an emotion or emotional pattern

Further Thoughts: In Life Coaching, metafeeling is also a common point of discussion. Outside of the coaching session, metafeeling tends to be a more common experience for the client even if he has never heard the word. For instance, the client often comes to the coaching process because he wants to feel more satisfied with the quality of his living, including the feeling he is doing as part of that living. This desire for more satisfaction with other feelings is a metafeeling.

Your role as the coach is to help the client address his feelings about his feelings. One of the most common questions used to do this is simply, "How do you feel about that?" An example when this inquiry is actually a metafeeling inquiry would be when you ask the client how he feels about his current level of happiness. If he says, "Happy with it" or "Disappointed," he has just shared with you a feeling about his feeling life.

The client's role in this process is to be open to learning what metafeelings tell him. Often, metafeelings are focused on satisfaction with other feelings. In some cases, problematic metafeelings can be a contributing factor in mental health issues. Individuals who are depressed are often chronically sad about their basic experience of sadness. If a client chronically reports sadness, worry, and frustration and showcases strong feelings about these feelings, a referral to a mental health professional may be in order.

Related Terms/Phrases:
Metaemotion
Metasentiment

First Appearance: Sixth sentence in the fourth paragraph of Determination Letter 1. Determination Letter 1 opens with, "Now is the tricky part." The fourth paragraph begins with, "Now might be a good time...." The sixth sentence starts, "Have you progressed to...." (p. 19)

## Metaphor

Definition – A figure of speech in which a word or phrase is used in its literal form to describe an object, idea, experience, or process

Further Thoughts: In Life Coaching, metaphors are a frequent part of the conversation. This is because metaphors and similes, which perform a similar function but use the word like, are a frequent part of everyday communication. Metaphors belong to the fabric of comparing and contrasting ideas, feelings, and experiences that makes up human thinking and dialogue.

Your role as the coach is to note when the client uses metaphors and to use those same metaphors, especially the ones that are frequently repeated verbatim or in theme, in the coaching conversation. One way to make sure the client's metaphors take center stage is to refrain from introducing metaphors of your own. This is where the use of clean language comes in.

The client's role in the use of metaphors is to speak naturally and learn from natural speech. When the client is feeling frustrated, more aggressive metaphors might come forth. When the client is feeling happy, metaphors might be of a bubbly nature. Regardless of what is gleaned, metaphors represent a rich form of communication that provides both you and the client with a wealth of information to work with. Over time, the client will learn to recognize and appreciate her own particular patterns of communication and use those patterns to help herself achieve her dreams.

Related Terms/Phrases:
Analogy
Comparison
Figure of Speech
Substitution

First Appearance: In plural form. First sentence in the third paragraph of Action Letter 4. Action Letter 4 opens with, "You are graduating from training...." The third paragraph begins, "Or are you more aware...." The first sentence is the beginning of the third paragraph and thus has the same start as the paragraph itself. (p. 30)

## Metathinking

Definition – Idea about an idea or ideational pattern

Further Thoughts: In Life Coaching, metathinking is a constant presence and process. You as the coach are constantly thinking about the client's thinking and using the information gleaned to support the client and further the success of his dreams and goals.

You can do this in many ways. Making observations about the client's thoughts and thinking patterns is one. Asking questions about the client's thoughts and thinking patterns is another. The balance you are trying to achieve as the coach is to use this tool to further your understanding as well as the client's understanding of her thoughts and thinking patterns as well as to move the process along.

The goal of metathinking is to grow and enhance thinking so that thinking can grow and enhance the client's life. Therefore, it is important that metathinking not be used to dissect every single notion that pops into the client's head but rather to explore those ideas that would benefit the client to explore.

Coaching sessions early on may be populated with overt metathinking, where you are actively sharing your observations with the client and the client is actively sharing his ideas with you. Later, metathinking might become more of a silent tool, one you check in with and the client checks in with to further conversation, but which is not discussed in any detail.

Related Terms/Phrases:
Metacognition
Metaidea

First Appearance: Fifth sentence in the third paragraph of Determination Letter 1. Determination Letter 1 opens with, "Now is the tricky part." The third paragraph begins with, "'Decisions, decisions,' is a common...." The fifth sentence starts, "Other days, it will question the truth...." (p. 19)

## Middle

Definition – The central portion of the Life Coaching session during which the majority of the work is done; also, the central portion of the Life Coaching relationship

Further Thoughts: In Life Coaching, the middle of the session is where the day's coaching conversation resides. In the beginning of the session, previous homework is checked in with and the topic for the day is chosen. At the end of the session, new homework is finalized and the client's participation in progress throughout the session reviewed.

In the middle of the session, your role as the coach is to listen to the client and help her explore what she wants to work on outside of the session as well as what her next steps will be. Possibilities are often put forth by the client and seriously considered by you and her. Your goal is to facilitate the client's selection and creation of goals. Ideally, if you are doing your job well in this portion of the session, it might look as though you are doing nothing at all.

The client's role in this portion of the session is to be an active participant. Rather than awaiting the delivery of answers and approaches, she should be creating them herself. As her time in coaching approaches the middle and eventually exits it, she will become more and more comfortable with this process and more and more adept at coaching herself.

Related Terms/Phrases:
Center
Meat of the Conversation

First Appearance: Fourth sentence in the ninth paragraph of Action Letter 4. Action Letter 4 opens with, "You are graduating from training...." The ninth paragraph begins, "Would a visualization...." The fourth sentence starts, "Can you imagine what your ideal...." (p. 30)

## Mindfulness

Definition – The state of being aware and open to awareness

Further Thoughts: In Life Coaching, being mindful is a tool that is often used by you the coach and the client. Mindfulness may have to be taught at first as it has not been encountered and is not understood by everyone. Mindfulness techniques and exercises might also have to be explored and assigned in order for it to become a natural part of coaching and the coaching process. Meditation is one such exercise.

Your role as the coach is to enhance the client's awareness of himself and his life. An increased understanding of his thoughts, feelings, and behaviors is often a central part of the client's increased familiarity with himself. Thus, an initial mindfulness step might be for you to ask the client to begin noting his thoughts, feelings, and behaviors along with any patterns that reveal themselves along the way. In addition, you will be charged with being mindful of your own presentation and effect on the client throughout the coaching session and relationship, tailoring your approach to suit the client as is required.

The client's role in mindfulness is to be open to being aware of who he is, what he wants, and what he has achieved. This requires the client to take stock of his life, not just give it a cursory glance. Therefore, it can be said that the client must pay more attention to himself and his life than he is accustomed to doing in order to be mindful. Focusing on the present will likely be one of the biggest challenges of mindfulness for the client as the pace of modern life often propels people to focus on the future.

Mindfulness is frequently a precipitate to appreciation. So, by increasing a client's ability to be mindful, you are also helping the client become better able to see and be satisfied with who he already is and what he already has.

Related Terms/Phrases:
Awareness
Consciousness
Perception

First Appearance: Third sentence in the twentieth paragraph of the Renewal Letter. The Renewal Letter opens with, "Having a Life Coaching business...." The twentieth paragraph begins, "Or maybe you want...." The third sentence starts, "So they can show their classes...." (p. 43)

## Mirror

Definition – To reflect or mimic

Further Thoughts: In Life Coaching, mirroring occurs in many different ways. Traditionally, mirroring was thought of in terms of the mirroring of body language. In fact, when people are connected, they often mirror each other's movements. In Life Coaching, mirroring goes beyond just a focus on body language to include the mirroring of thoughts, feelings, energy, and, when appropriate, behaviors.

Your role as the coach is to engage mirroring when it will be of benefit to the client. Reflecting back what a client has said or what the client is emoting through words and voice tone is one form of mirroring. Allowing your movements to follow and mimic those of the client is another.

Mirroring energy is one of the most helpful applications of mirroring in coaching. It often helps the process to approach the issue at hand with the same level of engagement that the client is exhibiting. A chipper client often likes to talk and work with an optimistic and enthusiastic coach. Of course, there are times when the opposite is true, when the client would best benefit from a dissimilar approach in order to provide balance.

The client's role is to behave naturally and to be open to connecting with you during coaching. The client will likely signal connection through mirroring of her own. In fact, as part of learning, the client will likely parrot back what you said to make sure she has heard you correctly, which is a form of reflection and mimicking that will help her to expand her understanding and awareness.

Related Terms/Phrases:
Copy
Emulate
Mimic
Parrot
Reflect


First Appearance: Fourth sentence in the twentieth paragraph of the Renewal Letter. The Renewal Letter opens with, "Having a Life Coaching business...." The twentieth paragraph begins, "Or maybe you want...." The fourth sentence starts, "So they can help their students...." (p. 43)

## Motivation

Definition – The drive or commitment to complete a task or engage in a process

Further Thoughts: In Life Coaching, motivation is often a topic of conversation or focus of work. The client is likely to come to the process with motivation, or more precisely the lack thereof, as a pre-identified stumbling block. Sometimes, motivation issues relate to getting things started, sometimes to keeping things going, and sometimes to ending them so something else can be started.

Your role as the coach is to assess the client's motivation, especially as it relates to identified goals and objectives. Your role is also to let the client know that feeling motivated is not a prerequisite to good work and progress. Too often, the client might think he has to be raring to go every step of the way or his life is doomed. This is not the case. When it would benefit the client to increase motivation, then working on ways to access and increase the client's perceived drive and commitment to his goals and life becomes a topic of discussion.

The client's role is to learn to do the work he needs to do when he feels motivated and when he doesn't. By removing feeling unmotivated as a stumbling block, the client exponentially increases his consistency and, therefore, his ability to make gains.

Related Terms/Phrases:
Eagerness
Energy
Inclination

First Appearance: Third sentence in the third paragraph of the Legacy Letter. The Legacy Letter opens with, "We meet at...." The third paragraph begins, "You have helped people...." The third sentence starts, "Helping them source...." (p. 47)

# Need

Definition – A physiological or psychological prerequisite for a person's survival or well-being

Further Thoughts: In Life Coaching, the word need is used in two primary ways. First, biological needs, also known as physiological needs, refer to those physical essentials that sustain the client's ability to exist. Food, shelter, and clothing are the most often cited needs in this case. The second way in which the word need is used takes the word well-being into account. The client can exist without ever attaining true well-being. This, of course, is not Life Coaching's aim. Thus, most of Life Coaching is geared toward these higher order needs.

Your role as the coach is to help the client understand the difference between basic needs and higher order needs. Whereas basic needs are delineated by the human body, higher order needs are determined by a client's particular values, wants, and wishes. Thus, the first thing a client must do and the first thing you must support the client in doing is identifying her needs. Then, the goal becomes to create paths and avenues for meeting such needs.

The client's role in this process is to take personal stock of herself and her life so that she is identifying and sharing what is true for her, not what sounds good. Identifying these types of needs, those that transform life from a chore to an enjoyable experience, can be difficult and make the client feel vulnerable, especially since preference and identity are often involved. Thus, she may ask for support from you, either overtly or covertly. It is your job to guide her to be able to support herself with less and less help from you over time.

Related Terms/Phrases:
Essential
Necessity

Prerequisite
Sustenance

First Appearance: In plural form. First sentence in the eighth paragraph of the Renewal Letter. The Renewal Letter opens with, "Having a Life Coaching business...." The eighth paragraph begins, "You may have heard of...." The first sentence is the beginning of the eighth paragraph and thus has the same start as the paragraph itself. (p. 41)

## Open

Definition – A state of being ready and available to experience or learn; willing to listen and consider or accept and address

Further Thoughts: In Life Coaching, both you and the client must be open to the process. In order for coaching to be its most effective, you and the client must be willing and ready to be affected by and to affect the coaching conversation. Through the creation of the Thinking Space, you and the client collaborate to create a space where both old and new are welcomed, where both familiar and foreign are blended to create effective measures and paths for transitioning the client from surviving to thriving.

Your role as the coach is to foster the client's openness as well as to remain engaged with your own. By adopting a beginner's mind, by being comfortable with not having all of the answers, you demonstrate that you are a constant student of life. By adapting and growing yourself, both as a coach and as a person, you pave the way for the client to accept transformation as a necessary and important part of the process.

The client's role is to be willing to change. No one emerges from coaching exactly the same as when they entered. Thus, the client must accept that doing things differently, thinking differently, and feeling differently will be a part of his journey as well. In fact, transitioning and transforming are the exact reasons he came to coaching in the first place.

Related Terms/Phrases:
Accepting
Embracing
Responsive

First Appearance: Fifth sentence in the twentieth paragraph of the Renewal Letter. The Renewal Letter opens with, "Having a Life Coaching business…." The twentieth paragraph begins, "Or maybe you want…." The fifth sentence starts, "So those being trained…." (p. 43)

## Open-Ended Question

Definition – An inquiry that requires more than a yes or no answer

Further Thoughts: In Life Coaching, open-ended questions are the rule, not the exception. They are the means by which you as the coach can better learn the client and her way of thinking, feeling, and being in the world. They are also the way you can help her move along from where she is to where she wants to go.

Open-ended questions take many forms. Their primary purpose is to engage the client's thinking, knowledge, and wisdom. The best coaching questions are powerful by nature. The best of those are transformational.

Your role as the coach is to ask questions, lots of them, and to know when to use which ones. You will use open-ended questions when you want to hear more from the client and when you want the client to hear more from herself. The use of open-ended and powerful questions is not just for your benefit, but for the client's as well. Such inquiries are portals to the client's inner world. They make the internal external and, therefore, capable of being observed and understood.

The client's role in the use of open-ended questions is to answer and ask them herself. Then, she must listen to the responses given and use the information gleaned to better her life and advance her dreams.

Related Terms/Phrases:
Advancing Question
Facilitating Question
Thought-Provoking Question

First Appearance: In plural form. Second sentence in the nineteenth paragraph of the Renewal Letter. The Renewal Letter opens with, "Having a Life Coaching business...." The nineteenth paragraph begins, "Or maybe you would like...." The second sentence starts, "To show new coaches how...." (p. 43)

## Opportunity

Definition – A chance for growth or advancement

Further Thoughts: In Life Coaching, opportunities abound. The coaching process is, in itself, an opportunity for the client to make changes to himself, his present, and his future. The goal of Life Coaching is to enhance the positives in the client's life and to introduce those things that he believes he are lacking.

Your role as the coach is to help the client recognize the presence of opportunities and create ways to successfully navigate them. In addition, your role is to help the client reframe stumbling blocks and other challenges to his progress into opportunities. In this way, the phrase, "What doesn't kill us makes us stronger," is converted into, "What doesn't stop us furthers our success."

The client's role is to be on the lookout for opportunities and to approach them with an open and inviting spirit. In addition, the client can benefit from being willing to look at challenges and difficulties in a different way, as a means to grow and learn, rather than just as pesky annoyances.

Related Terms/Phrases:
Alternative
Chance
Opening
Option
Shot

First Appearance: First sentence in the second paragraph of the Pre-Contemplation Letter. The Pre-Contemplation Letter opens with, "You might be wondering…". The second paragraph begins, "What is important is this…." The first sentence is the beginning of the second paragraph and thus has the same start as the paragraph itself. (p. 4)

## Passion

Definition – A strong interest or devotion

Further Thoughts: In Life Coaching, passion is a key ingredient in the conversation and the process. The client comes to coaching to find out what she most wants, work toward getting it, or both.

Your role as the coach is to assist the client in discovering her passion if she does not already know what it is. You may also be called upon to help the client feel more comfortable about making her life her own. It is not uncommon for the client to feel guilty about moving away from doing what she has been told to do her whole life to doing that which brings her joy. In supporting the client with this, you can help her see that she is not shirking responsibility, just transferring it from some-thing that she tolerates to something that she loves.

You will also be responsible for helping the client strategize how to make her passions a reality. This involves creating accountability measures, designing action plans, and regularly tracking progress. If the client encounters any stumbling blocks, you can both support and assist her in overcoming them.

The client's role in addressing passion is to discover what hers is and act upon it if she wishes. Or to act upon them if they are multiple. By being open to the coaching process, she is increasing the chance that she can have all she's ever wanted.

Related Terms/Phrases:
Interest
Leaning
Pursuit

First Appearance: In plural form. First sentence in the fourth paragraph of the Renewal Letter. The Renewal Letter opens with, "Having a Life Coaching business...." The fourth paragraph begins, "It's a tricky balance at times...." The first sentence is the beginning of the fourth paragraph and thus has the same start as the paragraph itself. (p. 41)

## Past

Definition – A period of time that has already come and gone

Further Thoughts: In Life Coaching, the past is only accessed when it directly impacts the present or the future. Work in the past is geared towards bringing successes forward and understanding the role of the client's learning history in the development of his core beliefs.

Your role as the coach is not to dig around in the client's past. Rather, you use the pertinent bits and pieces offered to facilitate the client's movement toward achieving his goals and dreams. One of the likely times the past will be briefly discussed is when explaining the role of learning history in creating core beliefs. Since limiting core beliefs are likely to be a stumbling block at some point, it is helpful for the client to know that these unhelpful beliefs were likely formed in childhood with lesser logic.

The client's role in addressing the past is to use information from it to help him create the future he wants. Disappointments and moments of satisfaction are mined for what they tell the client he would like now. Then, the necessary plans are made and the work toward progress ensues.

Related Terms/Phrases:
Days Gone By
History
Yesterday
Yesteryear

First Appearance: Third sentence in the sixth paragraph of Contemplation Letter 1. Contemplation Letter 1 opens with, "Your journey to becoming a Life Coach…." The sixth paragraph begins, "Why has your mind suggested…." The third sentence starts, "Something connected to a positive…." (p. 5)

## Pattern

Definition – A consistent or habitual approach; a reliable set of traits or characteristics

Further Thoughts: In Life Coaching, patterns are often discovered and created. Patterns may take the form of stumbling blocks and limiting beliefs or they may take the form of helpful habits and motivating rituals. They may move the client along or they may hinder progress.

Your role as the coach is to note patterns and discuss them with the client when appropriate. You may need to help the client curtail a set of habits that are impeding her success or to maximize a regular approach that is key to her progress. Creating an effective schedule is one type of pattern you may be called upon to assist in developing. This is especially true for the client who has difficulty with time management or staying motivated. Eliminating time wasters may be your duty when it comes to reducing unhelpful patterns.

The client's role in relationship to patterns is to identify what hers are. She can then keeps those that are of aid and get rid of those that are not. Effective habits and approaches are keepers; ineffective ones are not. Those patterns that drain energy and de-motivate are of special importance as their elimination often improves progress tenfold.

Related Terms/Phrases:
Custom
Habit
Ritual
Routine
Schedule
Trademark

First Appearance: In plural form. Fourth sentence in the eighth para-graph of Contemplation Letter 2. Contemplation Letter 2 opens with, ""Your mind may be filled with…." The eighth paragraph begins, "Are you ready to delve…." The fourth sentence starts, "To provide tools for replacing…." (p. 7)

## Pause

Definition – A temporary break or time-out from a task, process, or conversation

Further Thoughts: In Life Coaching, there is a significant focus on forward movement. Therefore, in order to be most effective, Life Coaching must also incorporate the pause. The pause is meant as a time for progress to be noted and appreciated, lessons to be crystallized and generalized, and being to overtake doing.

Your role as the coach is to help the client understand the purpose of the pause and to utilize it when necessary. Rather than approaching a newly emerged stumbling block with vigor, the client might want to think his way around the issue. Rather than jump from one project to the next, the client might want to acknowledge how far he's come. Rather than work, the client might want to play. Rather than do, the client might want to be mindful and soak up the beauty of his environment. The pause ensures that the client is not just a ball of action without purpose, but a human being who is living the life he dreams.

The client's role in using the pause is to uncover when it is most effective for him to engage. He may find that he needs to pause before the final step in a procession or take a moment prior to the first. He may find that the pause can help him channel his energy or even that it can aid him in creating it. There are no limits to the usefulness of the pause. Thus, the client must learn what the pause is to him and when to implement it so it, too, can enrich his life.

Related Terms/Phrases:
Break
Interlude
Recess

First Appearance: First sentence in the seventeenth paragraph of Contemplation Letter 6. Contemplation Letter 6 opens with, "You may be wondering, ' How many choices....'" The seventeenth paragraph begins, "Let's take a pause...." The first sentence is the beginning of the seventeenth paragraph and thus has the same start as the paragraph itself. (p. 17)

## Permission

Definition – Consent

Further Thoughts: In Life Coaching, you are charged with asking for the client's permission in many ways. One of the most common is when you would like to introduce content into the session. Since Life Coaching is a process by which the client's thoughts are furthered and enhanced, you do not want to do anything that would derail them in any way. This introduction of content may come in the form of feedback, an anecdote, or an approach. Asking permission does not have to be complicated. It can come in the form of a question as simple as, "I have a thought. Would you like to hear it?"

Though it is not often that the client will say no as she has come to the coaching process to learn and grow, on occasion, she will decline to give her permission. Making her feel comfortable about this is an important task that falls at your feet as a coach.

The client's role in the permission process is to be honest. If she is delving deep into a thought process and afraid she will lose her way if she accepts feedback at a particular juncture, it is important that she decline the new content. Often, it takes time for the client to become comfortable with the permission process. With your support, she will get there more quickly.

Related Terms/Phrases:
Approval
Nod of the Head
Yes

First Appearance: Sixth sentence in the twentieth paragraph of the Renewal Letter. The Renewal Letter opens with, "Having a Life Coaching business…." The twentieth paragraph begins, "Or maybe you want…." The sixth sentence starts, "So new coaches can understand…." (p. 43)

## Play

Definition – To engage in a task, process, or life in a way that is fun and produces joy

Further Thoughts: In Life Coaching, it is okay to play. This may be a concept that is difficult to understand when you consider that a client is paying you for a service. But play can be a service in itself.

Your role as the coach is to introduce or allow for play that facilitates the meaningfulness of the coaching conversation and the effectiveness of the coaching process. Play is an aid. It often helps the client become more comfortable and act more like his true self. For some clients, play is difficult. If your client does not wish for it to be a part of the coaching session, it is best to put play on the shelf. The likelihood is he will want it pulled back down again at some point.

The client's role in play is to engage in being lighter and freer. Whether play takes the form of a small joke or a fun assignment, the client benefits most from play when he participates in it. Over time, as he becomes more comfortable with the process, the client is likely to introduce play on his own.

Related Terms/Phrases:
Fun
Humor
Lightheartedness

First Appearance: Fourth sentence in the eighteenth paragraph of the Renewal Letter. The Renewal Letter opens with, "Having a Life Coaching business…." The eighteenth paragraph begins, "Maybe you want to write…." The fourth sentence starts, "To illustrate the use of…." (p. 43)

## Powerful Question

Definition – An inquiry that is thought-provoking and moves the coaching process forward

Further Thoughts: In Life Coaching, asking powerful questions is one of the four pillars of the coaching process, alongside listening, creating accountability, and designing action plans. Asking powerful questions is one of the skills that takes the most practice.

In asking a powerful question, as a coach, you must not only create the question but know when to ask it. The goal of a powerful question is to enhance the client's thinking. From this enhanced understanding, she can better know herself and how to turn her dreams into a reality.

There are many types of powerful questions. Some seek to ascertain a deeper understanding of fact, others to get the client in touch with being, still others to have the client recognize and further explore what she has just said. Powerful questions often end with the client bringing into her conscious awareness ideas and beliefs that previously only existed in her unconscious.

The client's role in the use of powerful questions is to respond to them and then eventually be able to ask them herself. As the client becomes more comfortable hearing and answering powerful questions, she learns that they are not only useful when asked by the coach, but helpful when she can come up with and ask them herself. This is a key shift in coaching as it is when the client begins to facilitate her own thinking in a deep and meaningful way.

Related Terms/Phrases:
Facilitating Question
Thought-Provoking Question
Transformational Question

First Appearance: In plural form. Third sentence in the nineteenth paragraph of the Renewal Letter. The Renewal Letter opens with, "Having a Life Coaching business...." The nineteenth paragraph begins, "Or maybe you would like...." The third sentence starts, "To demonstrate the form and use...." (p. 43)

## Present

Definition – The period of time that is happening now

Further Thoughts: In Life Coaching, the present is the time in which all action takes place. One way to look at the phases of time and a person's relationship with them is this: You can learn from the past, act in the present, and prepare for the future. There is no other order in which these things can be done. In fact, trying to do the above in a different order can create difficulty in a person's life.

Your role in working with the present is to follow the model above. You can assist the client in bringing forth successes and knowledge from his past that will help him achieve what he wants to achieve in the future by assisting him in working towards those wishes now, in the present. In addition, you can model and encourage mindfulness, which is a powerful approach to being aware of and interacting with the here and now.

The client's role in regard to the present is to live within it, rather than getting hung up on the past or spending too much time dreaming about the future. The fact is: Dreams are important, but they only became a reality if they are turned into goals and the requisite work is done to reach them. Also, the past is important but only in its capacity to enhance the experience or appreciation of the present. The present is all the client can experience, all that is available to him at any given moment.

Related Terms/Phrases:
Current Time
Here and Now
Today

First Appearance: Fifth sentence in the sixth paragraph of Contemplation Letter 1. Contemplation Letter 1 opens with, "Your journey to becoming a Life Coach...." The sixth paragraph begins, "Why has your mind suggest-ed...." The fifth sentence starts, "Is the why a coming together...." (p. 5)

## Process

Definition – A series of actions that produce a specific result or end

Further Thoughts: In Life Coaching, the process of how things are achieved is as much of a focus as what is to be achieved. Only through understanding and being part of the process can the client truly ensure success.

Your role as the coach is to help the client become comfortable with the process. One way to do this is to go over the importance of journey thinking versus destination thinking. Journey thinking recognizes that each step, from first to last, is as important as any other. Destination thinking bestows importance only on the last step, the one that closes the gap between not having and having. By helping the client see that understanding and appreciating the process is the key to replicating success, you are giving her access to a lifetime of accomplishments, not just supporting her in one.

In Life Coaching, effort is recognized and celebrated. The process is recognized and celebrated. The client's role is to learn why this is important and to utilize this approach to enhance her life and the attainment of her goals. By engaging with and acknowledging the importance of the process, the client will be positioned to achieve more than she ever thought possible.

Related Terms/Phrases:
Course of Action
How
Means
Method
Procedure
Ways

First Appearance: First sentence in the third paragraph of the Introduction Letter. The Introduction Letters opens with, "Somehow this book has found its way...." The third paragraph begins, "What follows are a series of letters...." The first sentence is the beginning of the third paragraph and thus has the same start as the paragraph itself. (p. 3)

## Progress

Definition – Movement toward or attainment of a goal

Further Thoughts: In Life Coaching, progress is measured not only in terms of goals achieved but effort expended. Trying is a form of progress, one that is far too often overlooked in everyday life.

Your role as the coach is to help the client understand just how many times progress shows itself along his coaching journey. By coming to coaching, the client has made progress. By engaging with the process, the client has made progress. By sharing and considering feedback, the client has made progress. By designing an action plan and agreeing to be held accountable, the client has made progress. In point of fact, there is no end to the client's progress in coaching; it is helpful for him to understand this.

The client's role in progress is to identify what kind he would like to make, work toward it, recognize when he is advancing, and utilize his progress to enhance his happiness and the satisfaction he has with his life. In coaching, by engaging with the process, the client is assured of making considerable progress.

Related Terms/Phrases:
Achievement
Advancement
Breakthrough
Improvement
Met Deadline
Met Goal
Movement Forward
Step in the Right Direction

First Appearance: Fourth sentence in the fifth paragraph of Action Letter 5. Action Letter 5 opens with, "Goals. Goals are the next stage...." The fifth paragraph begins, "How do you work with...." The fourth sentence starts, "In what way do you measure...." (p. 32)

## Purpose

Definition – A guiding force; a meaningful pursuit

Further Thoughts: In Life Coaching, the goal is for the client to live a life based on her purpose. You as the coach may even have seen or heard the phrase, "Living life on purpose."

Your role as the coach is to help the client get in touch with her purpose and live her life with it as a guiding force. This often involves values work. A client's purpose emanates from her values, those beliefs and motivations she holds most dear.

A client's values are her fuel. They are also her succor. They help her stay in touch with who she is and allow her to contribute to life in a meaningful way. They make her who she is and create for her a path to satisfaction and joy.

The client's role in regard to purpose is to pursue that which she treasures. She must start by exploring what inspires and sustains her. Then, she can forge from these elements a set of goals, ways to engage with herself, others, and life in a way that is enriching. By discovering her purpose and working from it, the client becomes the strongest she can ever be. She, in turn, experiences the most joy there is to have.

Related Terms/Phrases:
Aim
Aspiration
Desire
Dream
Hope
Objective
Value
Wish

First Appearance: Second sentence in the sixth paragraph of Contemplation Letter 6. Contemplation Letter 6 opens with, "You may be wondering, 'How many choices....'" The sixth paragraph begins with, "The ICF provides accreditation...." The second sentence starts, "It's the individual credentialing...." (p. 15)

## Referral

Definition – An instance where one professional recommends the services of another or sends a client to receive such services from the recommended professional

Further Thoughts: In Life Coaching, referrals are part of your responsibility as a coach. Sometimes, a referral is made when a client is seeking your services for the first time. Perhaps the client is really looking for therapy or mistook coaching for consulting. At other times, the client may ask you to add a type of service that you are not qualified to add, such as financial advising. Your role here is to recommend a type of service or a known professional for the client to see.

In the event that the client asks you to engage in a secondary service that you are qualified to provide, but which will result in an ill-advised dual relationship, then you will need to refer the client out for that service as well.

The client's role in the referral process is to take the information offered and make use of it if it is of benefit. The client always has the choice about whether or not to follow through on a referral. If the client is experiencing an issue that impacts his ability to benefit from coaching services, you may have to require that he seek out assistance before returning to coaching services. In addition, it is possible that certain services require the coaching process to be paused for a time. This is most often the case with a significant mental or physical health problem. In these instances, you cannot force the client to use your referral, but you can establish that you cannot maintain involvement as the coach if the problem at hand is not dealt with.

Related Terms/Phrases:
Recommendation
Suggestion

First Appearance: In plural form. First sentence in the fourth paragraph of Action Letter 6. Action Letter 6 opens with, "By now, you have set a few goals...." The fourth paragraph begins, "What is your plan...." The first sentence is the beginning of the fourth paragraph and thus has the same start as the paragraph itself. (p. 34)

## Reframe

Definition – To look at or consider a thought, feeling, behavior, situation, or process in a different way

Further Thoughts: In Life Coaching, reframing is a constant. The client frequently comes to the process to look at and live life differently. In addition, she is often looking for guidance on how to make and sustain change.

Your role as the coach is to help the client see things differently when to do so can be of benefit to her. You can do this by providing a fresh perspective when she seeks or is amenable to one. You can also teach her the process of reframing, which requires slowing down and looking at the situation from a different angle, often one guided by a different set of questions or ideas.

One of the biggest reframes in coaching is to see challenges as opportunities. This small shift results in freedom for the client as she can now see the different choices available to her and therefore make different decisions, ones that are in line with the direction in which she would like to go.

The client's role in the reframing process is to be open to learning about it and then using it both during the coaching session and in her life outside of the Thinking Space.

Related Terms/Phrases:
Approach from a Different Angle
Change Perspective
Reassess
Reconsider
Reevaluate
Reexamine
Rethink

First Appearance: First sentence in the fourteenth paragraph of Action Letter 4. Action Letter 4 opens with, "You are graduation from training...." The fourteenth paragraph begins, "To aid with this process...." The first sentence is the beginning of the fourteenth paragraph and thus has the same start as the paragraph itself. (p. 31)

## Relationship

Definition – A connection between two or more people; also, a connection between two or more thoughts, feelings, behaviors, situations, processes, or objects

Further Thoughts: In Life Coaching, the quality of the relationship between you and the client is the single most important factor in making the process successful. For coaching to work, you and the client must be a good fit for each other.

Your role as the coach is to initiate a positive connection with the client who has come to you for your services. You do this by showing the client respect and taking his dreams seriously. You also do this by helping to cocreate the Thinking Space. As part of the process of coaching, you will engage the four pillars – listening, asking powerful questions, creating accountability, and designing action plans – to assist the client in furthering his agenda so he can live the life he has always imagined.

The client's role is to work toward forging a professional connection with you. He can do this by being open to the procedures and dynamics of coaching and being his true self. Through his frequent sharing, he will become more intimately acquainted with himself as well as with what coaching can do for him. As a result, he will also feel connected to you and the services you have provided.

Related Terms/Phrases:
Association
Bond
Connection
Rapport

First Appearance: In plural form. First sentence in the fifth paragraph of Contemplation Letter 4. Contemplation Letter 4 opens with, "It's at this stage that you might be wondering...." The fifth paragraph begins, "For those looking to improve...." The first sentence is the beginning of the fifth paragraph and thus has the same start as the paragraph itself. (p. 11)

## Relaxation Technique

Definition – A method to create or induce a sense of calm or a lessening of tension

Further Thoughts: In Life Coaching, relaxation techniques are sometimes used or recommended for the client to use at home. In addition, some techniques with other purposes, such as visualization, can induce relaxation.

Your role as the coach is to incorporate relaxation techniques that you are qualified to use into the coaching process when it would be of benefit to do so. Most relaxation techniques are basic and meant for the client to use at home. Therefore, they do not require any training on your part. However, there are some, such as hypnosis, that should not be used without the proper education and practice. In addition, there are some, such as progressive muscle relaxation, that require approval from the client's physician.

When assigning relaxation techniques as a part of homework, it is often helpful to practice them first in a coaching session so that the client knows what she is supposed to do and is able to do it. Then, when it is clear the client is able to engage properly with the technique, she can be left to use it on her own.

Many mindfulness exercises bring about peace and relaxation even though their purpose is to create awareness. In the case of mindfulness techniques, even though it is possible to use most of them without any significant training, it is often helpful to attend a seminar, or at the very least read a book, to fully understand the philosophies behind them.

The client's role in relaxation techniques is to learn how and when to use them then to do so accordingly. The client may also choose to engage in expanding her repertoire of techniques outside of the coaching session via reading, watching videos, or attending classes or seminars. This is particularly true when relaxation is incorporated with exercise or mindfulness.

Related Terms/Phrases:
Calming Practice
Relaxation Exercise

First Appearance: First sentence in the tenth paragraph of Action Letter 4. Action Letter 4 opens with, "You are graduating from training...." The tenth paragraph begins, "Or is a relaxation technique...." The first sentence is the beginning of the tenth paragraph and thus has the same start as the paragraph itself. (p. 30)

**Reporting**

Definition – Sharing recent life events or current concerns, often in detail and typically at the beginning of a coaching session

Further Thoughts: In Life Coaching, reporting can be a helpful opening to a session. For the client, it often serves as a release valve as well as an opportunity to check in with thoughts related to recent events. Reporting can become an impediment to progress when it starts to take up the majority of the session.

Therefore, it is your job as the coach to move the client from reporting to the working phase of the session. This can be done in a supportive manner by asking thought-provoking questions. Reporting is more of a recap than an exploration. By providing the client with the opportunity to go deeper, true processing can begin.

For most clients, habitually spending too much time reporting is not an issue or is a temporary one if it is. However, there are some clients who cannot pull themselves out of the overreporting rut. In this case, you may need to explain the difference between reporting and processing and encourage the client to movie into working during each session for at least several sessions. Sometimes, time limits for reporting are necessary, too. When the client wants to gain the maximize benefit from the coaching conversation but cannot impose his own limits, having a specific cut off point can be helpful. One common guideline is that reporting should take no more than 15 minutes of a 60-minute session. Setting this kind of limit should always be discussed with and agreed upon by the client before implementation.

The client's role in reporting is to share a brief recap of pertinent information. Then, he is to transition to the thinking portion of the session.

Related Terms/Phrases:
Giving an Overview
Informing
Recapping
Summarizing
Updating

First Appearance: Seventh sentence in the twentieth paragraph of the Renewal Letter. The Renewal Letter opens with, "Having a Life Coaching business...." The twentieth paragraph begins, "Or maybe you want...." The seventh sentence starts, "So they can watch an experienced coach...." (p. 43)

## Request

Definition – An act of asking for something or something of someone; also, the act of such asking

Further Thoughts: In Life Coaching, requests are often made. As a coach, it is often best for you to formulate potential assignments as requests. This emphasizes the fact that the client can say no. Also, the word request is especially helpful when asking the client to step out of her comfort zone, as she will likely not feel as though she is being pushed. Request making is very much in line with the idea of offering invitations and identifying opportunities, both important aspects of coaching.

The client's role in requests is to learn to see them as opportunities as well as to make them of the coach when necessary. A client may request the opportunity to send an update email in between sessions. Or a client may request that the coach share with her a few extra reading resources on a topic that's been discussed.

The idea of making requests can also spill over into the client's life. This can be a positive bonus as requests have at their center respect for the person making them as well as the person receiving them. It is an example of the frequent positive ripple effect of coaching.

Related Terms/Phrases:
Ask For
Entreat
Petition
Present an Option

First Appearance: First sentence in the first paragraph of the Closing Letter. The Closing Letter opens with, "In closing, I find I want to make...." The first paragraph and the first sentence of the first paragraph are the same as the opening of the letter itself. (p. 48)

## Requirement

Definition – An essential resource or part of a process

Further Thoughts: In Life Coaching, a distinction can be made between a need and a requirement. A need, at its most basic level, is something a person must have to survive. A requirement, on the other hand, can be thought of as something a person must have to succeed. For example, the client may not need ten two-inch binders to live, but he may need those same binders to make the presentation he has planned.

Your role as a coach is to help the client learn to distinguish between needs, wants, and requirements as well as to understand that it is okay to have each in his life. For some clients, this is a difficult lesson. For others, it comes naturally. Part of your role in making this distinction is to gauge where the client is. Your client might collapse wants and requirements into needs, which can lead to the creation of unnecessary stumbling blocks as he may respond to the lack of a want being met or the inability to secure a certain resource as akin to navigating a threat to life. On the other hand, your client might eschew requirements and wants, often trying to go without, setting up impossible expectations that can never be met. For instance, if the client requires a certain amount of capital to fast track a project and he doesn't have it, he might start getting frustrated with himself because the project is taking longer on a tighter budget.

The client's role in dealing with requirements is to learn about them and be clear about them. Whether he is talking with you or someone outside of the coaching relationship, he needs to be clear about what he has to have to succeed.

Related Terms/Phrases:
Base Element
Essential
Fundamental
Prerequisite

First Appearance: In plural form. Third sentence in the eighth para-graph of Contemplation Letter 6. Contemplation Letter 6 opens with, "You may be wondering, 'How many choices....'" The eighth para-graph begins, "A lot already...." The third sentence starts, "The letters and requirements can be...." (p. 16)

## Resource

Definition – A supply; also, a supplier

Further Thoughts: In Life Coaching, the coaching process is the most fundamental resource the client has. It is a service that both gives and connects the client with the thing or things that she requires to succeed. Those things, those resources, can take many forms, from the concrete to the abstract.

Your role as the coach is to help the client access thinking resources first and foremost. Over time, through the coaching conversation, the client learns that she is the biggest resource she has. And her thoughts are a wellspring of purpose, pathways, and solutions. By learning to trust her mind and herself, the client becomes what she needs most.

The client's role in regard to resources is to recognize those that she already has and to develop or secure those that she still needs. Many of the resources that the client has come to the coaching process for are skills. Thus, skill building, especially in terms of thinking and thought processes, is essential to the success of coaching.

Related Terms/Phrases:
Ability
Foundational Element
Means
Necessity
Supporter

First Appearance: In plural form. Second sentence in the twelfth paragraph of Determination Letter 1. Determination Letter 1 opens with, "Now is the tricky part…" The twelfth paragraph begins, "On the cons side…." The second sentence starts, "They are likely comprised of…." (p. 20)

## Result

Definition – A consequence or outcome of an action, situation, or process

Further Thoughts: In Life Coaching, results are important. Though a lot of credence is given to effort throughout the process, the client does want something to come from the coaching conversation. What that something is depends on the client.

Your role as the coach is to understand what the client is looking for, what results he seeks. Then, through the creation of the Thinking Space and the use of Life Coaching techniques, you support him in achieving those wants.

The client's role is to be clear with himself and with you about what he is looking for. He must then put in the time and energy, both within and outside of the coaching session, in order to achieve those results.

Related Terms/Phrases:
Aftermath
Consequence
Development
Outcome
Payoff
Product
Return

First Appearance: Third sentence in the ninth paragraph of Action Letter 5. Action Letter 5 opens with, "I am curious...." The ninth paragraph begins, "Would it help to sit...." The third sentence starts, "To allow your mind...." (p. 32)

## Retainer

Definition – An amount of money due for access to a service or set of services for a specified period of time

Further Thoughts: In Life Coaching, retainers are common, especially for those coaches who work with corporations. The length of access to services with a retainer is typically one month or more. It is not uncommon for retainers to last for a year. Also, some coaches offer 24-hour access to their support via the purchase of a retainer. Clearly, such an offering is significantly more expensive than one that includes only a handful of coaching sessions. Also, 24-hour access retainers are often limited in number.

Retainers typically include not only sessions, but phone calls, video, and email access. For corporations, retainers frequently mean that you are on hand, available and waiting, for when they need you. Thus, you may not be required to provide any services for six months, but then you might need to spend a week working with the company to address its needs. For in-person services that require travel, it is important to specify who is responsible for the cost of travel and hotel accommodations. Many coaches build this in to their retainer fee.

Another popular fee schedule that is similar to a retainer is the package. This setup requires that a specific number of sessions must be purchased at a time and then used prior to their expiration. For example, you might require a new client to purchase four sessions so that she gets a chance to experience coaching for at least a brief period of time. Such a package can help keep her from suddenly stopping sessions if she hits a snag in her progress.

Your role as the coach is to decide if you would like to require a retainer for any or all of your services. Then, you must decide what to charge and for what services. It is important to keep in mind what you can accommodate. The client's role is to be aware of any retainer policies you have and to follow them if she has a retainer.

Related Terms/Phrases:
Payment Arrangement
Subscription

First Appearance: Sixth sentence in the tenth paragraph of Action Letter 6. Action Letter 6 opens with, "By now, you have set a few goals...." The tenth paragraph begins, "What are you seeking to make...." The sixth sentence starts, "Will you require your clients...." (p. 35)

## Risk

Definition – Chance, often with a possible lack of success or loss

Further Thoughts: In Life Coaching, risks are a necessary part of the process. In the case of the coaching process, risks are not meant to be dangerous. They are often simple, but still require flexibility and bravery. For instance, changes to thought, feeling, and behavior patterns are all risks. It is always possible that the new thoughts, feelings, or behaviors tried will not be as effective as the old ones.

Your role as the coach is to facilitate the client's willingness to engage with risks. Again, you are not supposed to push the client to do what he doesn't want to do. Rather, you are to discuss how doing something differently opens the door for an alternative result. Since the client has not come to coaching for his life or his self to remain the exact same way, this is an important part of the process.

The client's role is to become comfortable with taking risks. It is possible that your client may not like the word risk. This is not uncommon. In such a case, it is helpful to substitute the word chance or to use another synonym. The client benefits from being comfortable with the risk-taking process even if each individual risk or new step brings with it a little bit of apprehension as well as excitement.

Related Terms/Phrases:
Alternative
Chance
Invitation
New Approach
Opportunity
Possibility
Uncertainty

First Appearance: In plural form. Third sentence in the tenth paragraph of Action Letter 7. Action Letter 7 opens with, "I hear you have started…." The tenth paragraph begins, "There are so many aspects…." The third sentence starts, "There are risks to be…." (p. 36)

## Role

Definition – A function, behavior, or obligation or a set of functions, behaviors, or obligations associated with a certain demographic factor, profession, or relationship

Further Thoughts: In Life Coaching, the concept of roles is important. You as a coach have a certain role you must fulfill. This role is made up of many expectations and obligations defined by the vocation you have chosen. The client, too, has a role to follow. In the client's case, the role is to be an active participant in the coaching process and to work toward reaching the goals she sought your support for.

As the client progresses along the journey of coaching, the number and type of roles the client has will emerge. For instance, your client may be a business owner and a single mom and a member of the PTA. Or your client may be married with no kids but work part-time at a firm so she can still spend time caring for a disabled cousin.

In helping the client work toward her dreams, you will often have to help the client balance the responsibilities of one role with another. The client's relationship with and responsibility to herself will likely be one of her most overlooked roles, one that she is trying to address through the coaching process.

Related Terms/Phrases:
Duty
Expectation
Function
Obligation
Part
Responsibility

First Appearance: First sentence in the first paragraph of Action Letter 1. Action Letter 1 opens with, "With each new addition to your life...." The first paragraph and the first sentence of the first paragraph are the same as the opening of the letter itself. (p. 24)

## Role Conflict

Definition – Incompatibility or interference of a singular function, behavior, or obligation or a set of functions, behaviors, or obligations pertaining to a particular demographic factor, profession or relationship with that or those of another

Further Thoughts: In Life Coaching, the presence of role conflict will invariably arise. You will be tasked with helping the client identify when role conflict is occurring as well as support him in coming up with ways to address it.

The client will have many roles in his life. These roles will vary depending on his demographics, profession, and chosen relationships. For instance, the client may want to spend a weekend working on a professional project yet be responsible for taking his kids to sports practice. Or he may want to have a date night with his spouse, but need to visit his ailing parent at the hospital. There is no limit to the number and types of conflict that can occur between the client's roles. Also, there is no limit to the specific assumptions either the client, important people in his life, or society as a whole has for his roles. In fact, differences in role expectations are often a primary source of conflict in the client's life.

The client's role in addressing such conflict starts with being aware of what his roles are and the expectation for such roles, especially in terms of how such expectations and associated obligations impact his ability to work on his selected goals in Life Coaching. Then, he will have to address moments of conflict that have a significant impact on his progress or his satisfaction with the process by which he is attaining his dreams. Role conflict is often a source of guilt for the client; thus, he may turn to you for support in making himself a priority in his own life.

Related Terms/Phrases:
Difference of Opinion Regarding Obligations
Disagreement Over the Division of Labor
Discrepancy in Expectations

First Appearance: Third sentence in the first paragraph of Action Letter 1. Action Letter 1 opens with, "With each new addition to your life...." The first paragraph is the beginning of the letter and thus has the same beginning as the letter itself. The third sentence starts, "You will experience...." (p. 24)

## Routine

Definition – A regular or habitual pattern, course of action, or process

Further Thoughts: In Life Coaching, the client's routines often become a focus of conversation and work. The client, in pursuing her goals, will benefit from keeping those routines that aid her in moving forward and in replacing those patterns of thinking, feeling, and behaving that get in the way.

Your role as the coach is to help the client create approaches to goal attainment that benefit her and that work well in her current life. This help comes as a natural result of listening, asking powerful questions, creating accountability, and designing action plans. When significant changes to her personal habits are undertaken, the client may want to check in more often to discuss progress and address challenges. Setting up communication patterns that work for both you and her, such as check-in emails or phone contacts in between sessions, are part of your role as a coach.

The client's role in terms of routine is to evaluate what life patterns she has and address those that are not of benefit. As is the case with all other facets of Life Coaching, the client will discover there are approaches worth keeping and approaches worth tweaking or discarding. Committing to change is especially important when one habit is being altered or replaced by another because it takes time for a new pattern or process to take hold.

Related Terms/Phrases:
Everyday Method
Habit
Pattern
Regular Approach
Schedule
Standard Process

First Appearance: Second sentence in the second paragraph of Action Letter 7. Action Letter 7 opens with, "I hear you have started…." The second paragraph begins, "Have you had the chance…." The second sentence is, "To develop a routine?" (p. 36)

## Schedule

Definition – A plan or approach for a task or process involving the assignment of dates and times

Further Thoughts: In Life Coaching, scheduling is a significant part of the process. Not only do you as the coach schedule sessions and check-ins with the client, you also assist the client in carving out time to work on objectives outside of the coaching conversation.

Your role as the coach is to make sure that homework assignments and other follow-through measures are given their proper time and attention. You do this by helping to create accountability within the client's goals and by assisting in the development of action plans where goals are well-defined and achievable.

The client's role in scheduling is to make sure he works with you to keep sessions consistent so that the work done in them enhances his ability to reach his goals and dreams. In addition, he must help create ways to keep himself on track with moving forward with his objectives. This is done by breaking down larger tasks into smaller ones, assigning time to work on them, and following through with deadlines.

Related Terms/Phrases:
Agenda
Itinerary
Program
Timetable

First Appearance: First sentence in the sixth paragraph of Action Letter 2. Action Letter 2 opens with, "Now that you have decided...." The sixth paragraph begins, "Beyond the basics of learning...." The first sentence is the beginning of the sixth paragraph and thus has the same start as the paragraph itself. (p. 26)

## Self

Definition – Who a person is; a person's identity

Further Thoughts: In Life Coaching, the client's self is at the center of the process. The client often comes to coaching in order to engage in self-actualization. This means she is seeking to fulfill her potential, maximize her life satisfaction, and become the best version of herself possible.

Your role as the coach is to help the client get to know herself better especially in terms of what she wants for her life and, as a result, from the coaching process. You do this by listening, asking powerful questions, creating accountability, and designing action plans. Your role is supportive. It is also your responsibility to challenge the client to look deeper, past the societally delivered shoulds and ought tos, to what her core says she wants, what her values tell her she desires most.

The client's role in this process is to be open to discovering and communing with who she truly is. In order to do this, she may have to shed many layers composed of who she thought she should be or who others told her she ought to be. This can be a time of great vulnerability for the client as it requires her to take risks. As part of the process, she will think about, feel about, and do things differently. Thus, support, patience, and empathy will be important ingredients for success; she will need her own as well as some from you.

Related Terms/Phrases:
Being
Character
Identity
Individuality
Person
Personality

First Appearance: First sentence in the fifth paragraph of the Pre-Contemplation Letter. The Pre-Contemplation Letter opens with, "You might be wondering why…." The fifth paragraph begins, "This appreciation of self…." The first sentence is the beginning of the fifth paragraph and thus has the same start as the paragraph itself. (p. 4)

## Self-Actualization

Definition – The process of attaining a higher state of being in which a person has become his true self by reaching his full potential through living from his values and engaging his talents and abilities in his pursuits; also, the attainment of such a state

Further Thoughts: In Life Coaching, the desire for some form of self-actualization is what brings the client to the process. He wants more from life and from himself. This is why he seeks out your services to begin with. He may not have heard of the term self-actualization, a phrase coined by Abraham Maslow to describe the crowning destination of his original version of a human being's Hierarchy of Needs, but that doesn't mean he isn't familiar with the drive that Maslow said all humans have.

Your role as the coach is to help the client determine what self-actualization means to him. For every client, it is different. In order for your client to know what he wants, he must ask himself and he must listen. Self-actualization requires shifting from basic surviving to thriving. In fact, self-actualization is the pinnacle of thriving. It means the client has become all he has ever wanted to be. His life is now a realized dream.

The client's role in this process is to identify what he most wants and work toward achieving it. This involves him expanding his awareness of himself and his values as well as differentiating between the figurative voices of others in his head and his own inner voice. This process can ask a lot of the client. Therefore, it is helpful for him to understand self-actualization is very much a journey, not a destination.

Related Terms/Phrases:
Best Self
Highest Self
Self-Fulfillment

First Appearance: Third sentence in the eighth paragraph of the Renewal Letter. The Renewal Letter opens with, "Having a Life Coaching business…." The eighth paragraph begins, "You may have heard of…." The third sentence starts, "At the top of the pyramid…." (p. 41)

## Self-Care

Definition – The act or process of paying attention to and fulfilling one's own needs and wants

Further Thoughts: In Life Coaching, self-care is a significant sustaining factor for the client. In order to be at her best, she must make sure she is securing the resources she needs to survive, providing for the things she needs to succeed, and allowing herself access to at least her most significant wants.

Your role as the coach is to support the client in developing and maintaining effective self-care habits. On occasion, the client might slip in her self-care standards. If you notice this, it can helpful to point it out to her in a compassionate and empathic way. If the client develops significant issues with self-care, such as discontinuing proper hygiene maintenance, not getting adequate sleep over a long period of time, or not eating enough to maintain a healthy weight, it is likely that a health issue is at play and a referral is in order.

The client's role in self-care is to create basic self-care patterns that address needs, requirements, and wants, especially as they relate to goals she has set for herself as part of the coaching process. Then, she must regularly engage in self-care so that she can feel and function at her best.

Related Terms/Phrases:
Basic Hygiene
Looking After Oneself
Personal Care
Personal Health Maintenance
Self-Help

First Appearance: Third sentence in the twenty-third paragraph of Contemplation Letter 6. Contemplation Letter 6 opens with, "You may be wondering, 'How many choices....'" The twenty-third paragraph begins, "Thus, I will leave you...." The third sentence starts, "Feel free to engage in...." (p. 18)

## Self-Esteem

Definition – The regard, respect, or worth one has for oneself

Further Thoughts: In Life Coaching, self-esteem can either positively or negatively impact the process. The goal is for the client to have and maintain healthy self-esteem. Healthy self-esteem is self-regard that is based on a person's true attributes, abilities, and talents. Self-esteem that is too high or too low is not realistic; it does not adequately reflect who a person is or the worth that he has.

Your role as a coach is to address self-esteem as is necessary. Your primary relationship to the client's self-esteem will be in making sure he is aware of his abilities and talents and is using them in a way that moves him forward toward his goals. Small dips in self-esteem, such as doubting whether or not a dream can be accomplished or whether or not one has the resources to start or see a process through, are a natural part of life and can, therefore, be addressed as part of the coaching process. Significant issues with self-esteem require a referral to a mental health professional; they often accompany other mental health issues and are outside of your purview of training and experience.

The client's role in self-esteem is to develop and maintain a realistic picture of himself and his abilities. By knowing who he is and what he is capable of doing, he is better positioned to take on the tasks and responsibilities he is capable of, ask for help when he needs it, and delegate those items and steps that he does not have the skill set for. This is an especially important part of coaching for, as the poet John Donne once said, "No Man is an island, entire of itself."

Related Terms/Phrases:
Self-Confidence
Self-Respect
Self-Worth

First Appearance: Seventh sentence in the eighteenth paragraph of the Renewal Letter. The Renewal Letter opens with, "Having a Life Coaching business…." The eighteenth paragraph begins, "Maybe you want to write…." The seventh sentence starts, "To explore how being deeply…." (p. 43)

## Session

Definition – The time and space during which the coach and client engage in the coaching conversation

Further Thoughts: In Life Coaching, the majority of contact between you and the client occurs during a session. As a coach, you have many responsibilities in terms of sessions. To start, you must participate in their scheduling. You are also responsible for arriving to sessions on time, whether they be in person, by phone, or via video.

Of course, the majority of your responsibilities in a session revolve around creating and maintaining the Thinking Space. In order to do this, you must communicate your belief and interest in the client and provide her with the time and space she needs to adequately engage in and benefit from the coaching conversation. By listening, asking powerful questions, creating accountability, and designing action plans, you are providing the client with the services she seeks and helping her to better herself and her life so that she can thrive and be joyful.

The client's role also begins with working with you to schedule sessions at a rate and with a distance in between that allows her to stay in adequate contact with the process, work towards her goals, and benefit from what she is learning about and from herself. From there, she must actively participate in each session, making sure to be open and honest about what she wants and needs. She must also participate in designing next steps and following through on her commitments.

Related Terms/Phrases:
Appointment
Coaching Conversation
Meeting

First Appearance: Second sentence in the twelfth paragraph of Contemplation Letter 3. Contemplation Letter 3 opens with, "At this stage, you may be wondering…." The twelfth paragraph begins, "And, in the process, Life Coaching transforms…." The second sentence starts, "Each session of Life Coaching…." (p. 10)

## Session Note

Definition – Documentation of a coaching session that includes, at minimum, who was seen; the date, time, and length of the session; and a general overview of what was worked on

Further Thoughts: In Life Coaching, each session requires an accompanying session note. The purpose of the session note is to prove that a service has taken place as well as to provide you with an overview of the coaching process and relationship. By having a written summary of the client's services, you are able to check in with the work you have already done as well as the expectations the client has set for the process. One of the most helpful portions of keeping a session note is being able to document and then reference the specifics of homework assignments. This is a great asset in creating and maintaining accountability for the client.

As the coach, you are responsible for creating the session note. It is possible that the client might wish to see at least one session note to better understand what session notes are. It is often helpful to have the client read the session note during a session so he can ask you any questions he has about its set up or what you have written.

A session note does not have to be long. Its purpose is to allow you to stay in touch with what has occurred in each session. It is not meant to be a transcript of everything that has been said.

The client does not have any formal responsibilities in regard to the session note. If he requests a copy of his record, however, it would behoove him to know that he becomes responsible for maintaining the copies he has so that they remain confidential. Of course, any release or the client's record requires consent from the client and must be documented. If the client asks for his session notes to be released to another professional it is important that he understand that you have no control over how that professional handles documents. It is often helpful to discuss with the client that each release of his records increases the chance that there could be a slip in confidentiality.

Related Terms/Phrases:
Coaching Paperwork
Record of Service

First Appearance: In plural form. Sixth sentence in the eighth paragraph of Action Letter 6. Action Letter 6 opens with, "By now, you have set a few goals...." The eighth paragraph begins, "How many hours do you...." The sixth sentence is, "Session notes?" (p. 34)

## Shoulds

Definition – A type of core belief in which a person subscribes to a specific, unalterable way of thinking about, feeling about, and doing things that includes the anticipation of extreme consequences when expectations are not met

Further Thoughts: In Life Coaching, shoulds are a frequent stumbling block for the client. Every person alive has experienced or bought into shoulds at some point. When they are healthy, shoulds are thought of as possibilities or maybes. For instance, the client may think it best to get an A in a class in which she has the ability to get an A. She might see this as a positive contribution to her GPA or the result of thorough understanding.

A should is born when maybe becomes has to, when there is no other option, when rigidity takes center stage. Thus, when facing the same scenario, the client may tell herself she has to get an A in a class or she will fail out of school and live an unhappy life. As can be seen, the anticipated consequence is extreme. Getting a B in class, the first step down from an A, is not an academic threat. It will not lead to the client being kicked out of school. Getting a B is also not a harbinger of future unalterable misery.

Your role as the coach is to keep your eye out for shoulds and to challenge them when they get in the way of the client living a full and authentic life. Your primary focus in addressing shoulds will relate to those that are stumbling blocks along the client's path to reaching her dreams.

The client's role in addressing shoulds is to be aware of their existence, identify them when they have a negative impact on her progress, and replace them with more adaptive and flexible approaches.

Related Terms/Phrases:
Hard and Fast Rules
Musts
Ought Tos
Rigid Expectations

First Appearance: Eighth sentence in the twentieth paragraph of the Renewal Letter. The Renewal Letter opens with, "Having a Life Coaching business...." The twentieth paragraph begins, "Or maybe you want...." The eighth sentence starts, "So they know how to label...." (p. 43)

## Skill

Definition – An ability that arises from a natural talent, training, or a combination of the two

Further Thoughts: In Life Coaching, skills are discussed at length. The client is likely to choose goals that are in alignment with his strengths and abilities. In the event that he does not know what those are, then he will likely work toward discovering them as part of the coaching process.

Your role as the coach is to promote the use of skills that the client has and to develop those that are either untapped by or unknown to him. You can start by sharing with him any of your observations of his abilities. It is important that you understand that, just because a skill or talent seems obvious to you, it doesn't mean that the client is aware of it or its value to him. In this way you can help the client build his collection of skills, which is often referred to as a skill set in the field.

The client's role in regard to skills is to share with you those that he is aware of that can help further his progress toward his identified coaching goals. He would also benefit from being open to hearing about skills he has not identified as important or that he doesn't know he has. Finally, in order to achieve maximum success, he must be amenable to developing new skills.

Related Terms/Phrases:
Ability
Aptitude
Handiness
Know-How
Savvy
Talent

First Appearance: First sentence in the eleventh paragraph of Contemplation Letter 2. Contemplation Letter 2 opens with, "Your mind may be filled with thoughts...." The eleventh paragraph begins, "If consulting is what calls to you...." The first sentence is the beginning of the eleventh paragraph and thus has the same start as the paragraph itself. (p. 7)

## Solution

Definition – A specific answer to a problem or a method for successfully resolving an issue

Further Thoughts: In Life Coaching, solutions are part of the business. The person charged with generating solutions is the client. The person who is supposed to support the client in coming up with solutions is, of course, you – the coach.

Your role in finding solutions is supportive. While it is okay for you to contribute your thoughts and ideas when given permission or when asked, it is not your job to have all the answers. Life Coaching is very much about helping the client learn to master her own life and do things for herself rather than relying on having them done for her.

The client's role in relationship to solutions is to identify the challenges or stumbling blocks she wishes to address and then work toward resolving them successfully. She can ask for your help, but she is not to develop a dependence on it. You as the coach are a facilitator, not a guru. You and the client work collaboratively; you are not meant to shoulder the bulk of the load.

Related Terms/Phrases:
Adjustment
Antidote
Correction
Countermeasure
Fix
Remedy
Stopgap

First Appearance: Fourth sentence in the eighth paragraph of Action Letter 3. Action Letter 3 opens with, "I imagine your mind is…." The eighth paragraph begins, "The tools you have learned…." The fourth sentence starts, "It provides you with just enough…." (p. 29)

## Specialty

Definition – An area of focus and/or experience, often of both

Further Thoughts: In Life Coaching, you will decide which clients you want to serve and what you would like to work on with them in general. The areas that you choose to focus on in your coaching business are called your specialties. Common specialties include Business Coaching, Career Coaching, Executive Coaching, Health and Wellness Coaching, Leadership Coaching, Spiritual Coaching, and Transitional Coaching.

It is often recommended that you choose and advertise that you provide at least three in order to have access to a broad enough client base to support your business. As your career progresses and you build a loyal clientele, you might find that you really only need to focus on one. Of course, the choice is always up to you.

As far as your role goes, you will need to secure any training or mentor coaching necessary to make you proficient in the area in which you have chosen to work. At a minimum your training should include self-study via books. Often times, however, it will be of benefit for you to receive feedback on actual sessions from someone who knows how to do what you are doing. Depending on what you are working on and the competitiveness of the market that you are in, you may have to update your skill set on a regular basis to stay current and offer clients access to state of the art approaches, assessments, and/or tools.

The client's role in terms of specialty is to seek out a coach that works within the area that he is seeking assistance. In the event that he has chosen a coach who does not have experience and cannot attest to competence in the specialty area he requires, he must be amenable to seeking out services elsewhere.

Related Terms/Phrases:
Area of Competence
Area of Focus
Career Focus
Competency
Track
Type of Practice

First Appearance: Sixth sentence in the second paragraph of Contemplation Letter 4. Contemplation Letter 4 opens with, "It's at this stage that you might...." The second paragraph begins, "The Coaching experience is different for everybody...." The sixth sentence starts, "You, too, may invent...." (p. 11)

## Stage of Change

Definition – A regular and predictable response by a person to a shift or alteration in situation, circumstance, or experience

Further Thoughts: In Life Coaching, the client is likely to go through stages when facing and moving through change. There are typically five main stages of change, which are based upon the five stages of grief discovered by Elisabeth Kübler-Ross: Denial, Anger, Bargaining, Depression, and Acceptance. As a coach, you will not be expected to deal with these phases in a clinical way, but it may be helpful for you to recognize their milder cousins which may come up in coaching.

For instance, when a favored approach toward a goal does not consistently work, the client may insist that a change in method is not necessary. This is a form of denial. If the client cannot achieve results at the speed that she wishes to achieve it, she may become frustrated. This is a variation of anger. Her response, when faced with a significant setback or delay, may be to make small concessions, hoping that this will result in a return to the timetable she first envisioned. This is a form of bargaining. When her compromises do not result in the ends she envisioned, she may become disheartened. This is a type of sad, though not clinically depressed, mood. Eventually, through work and effort, she will learn to acknowledge her circumstances and work with them to achieve success. This is a form of acceptance.

Your role as a coach is to recognize the stages of change and provide the type of support necessary to each. What that is differs depending on the client, but any support offered must be compassionate, empathic, and in the client's best interest.

The client's role in addressing the stages of change is to learn what they are and the signs of each. She is then positioned to address them as needed.

Related Terms/Phrases:
Phase of Adaptation
Stage of Adjustment

First Appearance: In plural form. First sentence in the ninth paragraph of Action Letter 7. Action Letter 7 opens with, "I hear you have started…." The ninth paragraph begins, "Where are you in terms of…." The first sentence is the beginning of the ninth paragraph and thus has the same start as the paragraph itself. (p. 36)

## Strength

Definition – A talent, aptitude, or ability

Further Thoughts: In Life Coaching, strength identification and utilization are key to the client's success. The client will come to the coaching process with abilities that are either better than average in relationship to his other skills, better than average in relationship to others' abilities in the same area, or both.

Your role as the coach is to help the client identify his strengths and find ways to use them to reach his goals. If you like, you can use a strengths-based assessment such as CliftonStrengths. Or you can employ the use of any of an array of other aptitude tests. Of course, assessments are not required. Often, the coaching discussion is enough to assist the client in identifying enough skills and abilities so that the progress he seeks can be made.

The client's role in terms of strengths is to participate in identifying the ones he already has, developing ones that are latent but which can blossom with proper attention, and finding alternatives to those not in his power to grow to an effective potency.

Related Terms/Phrases:
Ability
Competence
Expertise
Skill
Savvy
Talent

First Appearance: In plural form. Third sentence in the eighth paragraph of Contemplation Letter 2. Contemplation Letter 2 opens with, ""Your mind may be filled with…." The eighth paragraph begins, "Are you ready to delve…." The third sentence starts, "To explore strengths…." (p. 7)

## Stretch

Definition – To extend oneself beyond what is typical

Further Thoughts: In Life Coaching, the client comes to the process to stretch. She seeks to take her life and herself beyond what has been. Your role as the coach is to help the client to figure out where she needs to stretch and to support her in the process. Since stretching is fundamental to the process of coaching, the basics are your tools: listening, asking powerful questions, creating accountability, and designing action plans.

The client's role is to share who she wants to be and what she wants to achieve. Then, with your help, where stretching is needed can be determined. Stretching might be necessary in the realm of thoughts. Or in the realm of feelings. Or in the realm of habits and other behaviors. Most of the time, stretching includes adding skills to the client's toolbox. In fact, this is one of the most common forms of stretching for a client – learning new ways to do things and using these new approaches when to do so increases the chance or expediency of success.

Related Terms/Phrases:
Adapt
Enrich
Expand
Grow
Learn

First Appearance: Sixth sentence in the second paragraph of the Renewal Letter. The Renewal Letter opens with, "Having a Life Coaching business...." The second paragraph begins, "You are evolving...." The sixth sentence starts, "Your mind might be drifting...." (p. 41)

## Stuck

Definition – To be or to feel unable to move forward

Further Thoughts: In Life Coaching, the client may come to the process feeling stuck. He may have many ideas about what he wants to do and the direction he wants to go but not be able to choose between them. Or he may be having trouble coming up with a plan or a dream that feels right, one that emanates from his core. Or he may know what he wants to do and in what direction he wants to go, but not be sure what the best route for getting there is. In essence, there are many ways in which the client can feel stuck.

Your role as the coach is to help the client notice when he feels stuck and to assist him in exploring this feeling. One of the most common signs you can watch out for as a coach is the lack of forward move-ment. When a client stalls, when he is no longer making strides toward his goals between sessions, he is likely feeling stuck.

By identifying the limiting beliefs behind his assumed inability to move forward, you can support him in coming up with ways to tackle the problem at hand or to move around it. In this way, blocks are trans-formed from progress-denying impediments to mere detours. Again, basic coaching methods are the means to address the client's sensa-tion of being stuck. The important thing is not to ignore it.

The client's role is to be honest with himself and with you about any hitches in his progress. The earlier he tells you about his trepidations with a plan or course of action, the less time this hiccup has time to build into something bigger in his mind. It is important that the client know that you expect there will be minor bumps in the road. He does not have to be perfect. No one does or can be.

Related Terms/Phrases:
Confused
Frustrated
Overwhelmed
Pulled in Two Different Directions
Uncertain

First Appearance: Seventh sentence in the second paragraph of the Renewal Letter. The Renewal Letter opens with, "Having a Life Coaching business...." The second paragraph begins, "You are evolving...." The seventh sentence starts, "Or you might be stuck...." (p. 41)

## Success

Definition – Favorable outcome of an attempt or set of attempts; attainment of a desired goal, position, or status; also, a person who has achieved

Further Thoughts: In Life Coaching, the client wants to succeed. At what and by what measure only she can say, but she does wish to reach a certain height or become a certain version of herself that makes her feel fulfilled. Thus, it is important that Life Coaching focus on helping the client get to where she is going.

Your role as the coach is to use your tools – listening, asking powerful questions, creating accountability, and designing action plans – to help her get there. Beyond these basics, the number and type of specialized tools you will use is up to you and your process as well as the client's wants and needs. You may wish to incorporate a strengths inventory to know what you and she have to work with. Or you may wish to incorporate an addendum to your intake that involves a more in-depth look at certain skills, such as time management and organization, depending on what your client's dreams are.

The client's role is to first define what success means to her. She must know what she wants and why she wants it. By understanding the why, by making sure what she chooses to pursue is in line with her values and those things that are most meaningful to her, she can ensure that her pursuits bring her satisfaction and joy, that they add to her life and enrich it. Then, once she is certain that what she has chosen to work on is what she wants most, she must put in the hours and the effort to make her dream come true.

Related Terms/Phrases:
Accomplishment
Achievement
A Dream Come True

Progress
Prosperity
Triumph

First Appearance: Third sentence in the twelfth paragraph of Contemplation Letter 5. Contemplation Letter 5 opens with, "It's good to see
you..." The twelfth paragraph begins, "Perhaps there is a certain...."
The third sentence starts, " A way to achieve...." (p. 14)

## Suffering

Definition – To be subject to pain or distress; to endure pain or distress

Further Thoughts: In Life Coaching, a client is not appropriate for services if he is dealing with significant thinking, feeling, or behavioral dysfunction. As has been made clear, mental health issues and their related functional impairments must be addressed by mental health professionals.

Thus, if your client exhibits signs of a mental health issue, your role is to refer out. Though it may seem like referring out isn't doing much for the client, it is, in fact, a tremendous service. Having somebody care enough to say, in a compassionate and empathic way, "I think you might need some help," is of major benefit. It is important, as a coach, that you know this, that you recognize this, and that you do the good that you can do in such a situation, which is to suggest to the client that he secure the services he needs.

The client's role in suffering is to get help. Whether he necessitates therapy, medication, or both, he should get assistance. Untreated mental health issues tend to compound themselves over time. They rarely get better spontaneously. The most severe kind never do, not without intervention. And though you cannot force a client to get help, suggesting that he speak with someone who can determine if he needs professional assistance and, if so, what kind would benefit him, is often the encouragement he needs to feel comfortable taking the next step.

Related Terms/Phrases:
Dysfunction
Functional Impairment
Mental Disorder
Mental Health Issue
Mental Illness

First Appearance: Fifth sentence in the eighth paragraph of Contemplation Letter 2. Contemplation Letter 2 opens with, ""Your mind may be filled with...." The eighth paragraph begins, "Are you ready to delve...." The fifth sentence starts, "To deeply explore...." (p. 7)

## Support

Definition – To assist or help sustain; also a person who helps another

Further Thoughts: In Life Coaching, support is a central part of the process. Your role as the coach is to support the client, to be a support for the client. You do this by helping to create the Thinking Space and engaging the client in meaningful conversation directed at helping her achieve her goals and dreams. You may also be called upon to challenge the client from time to time. It is easy to think of challenging as existing outside of the realm of coaching. But it does not. Challenging, when done with empathy and compassion, is the very essence of supportive assistance.

The client's role is to be open to receiving support. In general, she and you know she is coming to coaching in order to receive support. However, there may be times where she would like more support than others. It is her job to ask for it even though you will be keeping an eye out for such instances as the coach. It is also her job to provide feedback about the support she is receiving, especially if it is not meeting her needs.

Related Terms/Phrases:
Aid
Assist
Back
Encourage
Have Confidence In
Help
Serve

First Appearance: Fourth sentence in the fifth paragraph of Determination Letter 2. Determination Letter 2 opens with, "Here we are." The fifth paragraph begins, "If this is it, Young Life Coach…." The fourth sentence starts, "And know that I support…." (p. 22)

## Support Network

Definition – A group of individuals who provides assistance to another, either one-by-one or together

Further Thoughts: In Life Coaching, the client will often share who is supportive of him and his dreams. He will, over time, even without asking, mention those people who are most prominent in his life. However, it is often helpful to include a purposeful discussion about his support network.

Your role as the coach is to discuss the importance of having a support network as well as help him expand upon the ways he can engage with those who care about him most, especially in terms of his pursuit of life satisfaction. If, for any reason, there are gaps in the client's support network, it may be helpful to discuss with him methods by which he can plug those gaps. For instance, he may not be in contact with anyone who does what he is pursuing as a dream. Therefore, it might help him to network, to meet people who share his passion.

The client's role in regard to a support network is to share pertinent information about his in sessions. For example, during a discussion of an upcoming goal that is part of his action plan, he might disclose that he knows someone who is a computer whiz. His next endeavor might require building a website or creating an online marketing platform. In this case, he may be able to ask for and receive support from that person if he realizes that this is an okay thing to do.

It is possible for the client to fall into a rut, to think that he must do everything, complete every step on his own, for his dream to remain his dream. This is not the case. Also, helping him understand that it is not only okay but expedient to ask for help rather than only waiting for it to be offered is a critical service that you as the coach can provide.

Related Terms/Phrases:
Colleague
Family Member
Friend
Life Coach
Provider

First Appearance: Second sentence in the fifth paragraph of Action Letter 6. Action Letter 6 opens with, "By now, you have set a few goals...." The fifth paragraph begins, "Have you already identified people...." The second sentence starts, "New members you can add...." (p. 34)

## Surviving

Definition – To be adequately addressing the needs and requirements of every day living so as to prevent suffering

Further Thoughts: In Life Coaching, the client must at least be at the surviving level of existence. What this means is she must free be of major dysfunction and be able to get by okay. By surviving, she is not yet meeting her full potential.

Your role as the coach is to help her unlock her full potential. The dreams she wants to pursue and the talents she wants to develop are, of course, up to her. You can best be a support by cocreating the Thinking Space with her and using your skills as a coach – listening, asking powerful questions, creating accountability, and designing action plans.

The client's role is to participate in the coaching process. She can start by exploring and connecting with her values so she can decide upon and pursue the dreams and goals that are most meaningful to her and that will most enrich her life. Then, she must construct, with your help, the paths she will use to get where she needs to go and follow them. There is much work for her to do in order to for her to reach her destination. And there is much enjoyment of the journey along the way. It is this continued access to and appreciation of joy that will open to doors to thriving for her.

Related Terms/Phrases:
Doing Okay
Feeling Okay
Getting By
Making Ends Meet
Meeting One's Basic Needs
Plugging Along

First Appearance: Fourth sentence in the first paragraph of Contemplation Letter 3. Contemplation Letter 3 opens with, "At this stage, you may be wondering…." The first paragraph is the beginning of the letter and thus has the same beginning as the letter itself. The fourth sentence starts, "Anyone who wants to move beyond…." (p. 9)

## Talent

Definition – A pronounced strength or ability

Further Thoughts: In Life Coaching, the client will bring talents to the process. Often, however, the client is not aware of what his strengths are. This is a common occurrence in life and the reason there exist assessments and services designed to help people determine what they are good at and how to make use of such abilities.

Your role as the coach is to help the client discover his talents, especially those related to this goals and dreams. You may rely on discussion and observation or you may rely on tools to assist you along the way. If any of the measures you wish to incorporate into sessions mandates training, you will, of course, be responsible for securing such training prior to its use. Most of the exploration you will be doing will likely involve checking in with the client about how things are going. When adroitness at a particular task or approach comes to your attention, it is important that you share what you have observed, that you let the client know he is good at something, either in comparison to his other skills, in comparison to others, or both.

The client's role is to be willing to discover and use his talents to create his desired life. Those that he is aware of he should mention to you, especially if they are pertinent to what he wants to work on. Those that are as yet undiscovered he should be on the lookout for and be ready to embrace.

Related Terms/Phrases:
Ability
Aptitude
Gift
Strength

First Appearance: Third sentence in the second paragraph of the Renewal Letter. The Renewal Letter opens with, "Having a Life Coaching business...." The second paragraph begins, "You are evolving...." The third sentence starts, "You might be feeling on edge...." (p. 41)

## Teaching Moment

Definition – An opportunity to impart a lesson, often one that stems from and ties into current discussion or experience

Further Thoughts: In Life Coaching, teaching moments are a welcome opportunity. Though the majority of your role as a coach is to facilitate the client's thinking, you may be called upon, from time to time, to share something you know. That something may be a fact, a figure, an approach, a process, etc. There is no end to the type of teaching moments that might come up in coaching. The key is to ask permission before imparting a lesson.

When engaging in a teaching moment, especially when it is in the form of a correction or an attempt to help the client replace her standard way of doing things with something new, it is essential to start with a positive. Share something that shows you have recognized and have appreciated her effort and skill thus far. Explain that you have a small piece of information or a possible tweak that might exponentially increase the benefit she receives from her applied attention and effort. Then, remind her, after sharing what you meant to share, that the choice of whether to use what you have presented has always been and will always be with her. This can sound like a lot of pomp and circumstance. But it is essential in maintaining a collaborative relationship and keeping the client engaged as a mutual partner.

The client's role is to be open to teaching moments, both those encountered in the coaching relationship and those stumbled upon as a result of everyday living. The more the client learns to appreciate that she can, if she chooses, benefit from being a perpetual student of life and living, the better off she will be. Learners adapt; they seek to change. And the most successful people on Earth, the most innovative people on Earth are not those who turn down opportunities to learn something new, but those who embrace them.

Related Terms/Phrases:
Challenge
Learning Opportunity
Teachable Moment

First Appearance: Sixth sentence in the twentieth paragraph of the Renewal Letter. The Renewal Letter opens with, "Having a Life Coaching business...." The twentieth paragraph begins, "Or maybe you want...." The sixth sentence starts, "So new coaches can understand...." (p. 43)

## Testimonial

Definition – A statement or written declaration in support of a person or company or a person's or company's skills or offerings

Further Thoughts: In Life Coaching, unlike some other professions, it is okay for you as a coach to ask for testimonials from your clients. It is important, in doing so, that any client you ask be aware that he can always say no and that a no will not result in withdrawal of your support or the issuance of a penalty from you.

If you have a website, as a coach, it might be helpful to have the client post a testimonial there. Some search engines allow users to submit reviews, too. This is another place a client could place a testimonial. And, if you are credentialed by certain governing bodies in life coaching, clients can sometimes place reviews on their websites as well. Part of your role will be to determine where you would like positive reviews to be posted, keeping in mind that the primary goal of such reviews is, of course, to generate business.

The client's role, if he chooses to provide you with a testimonial, is to be honest and share what has been of most benefit to him from your service. Today, people who read reviews are very savvy. They can often tell when a rating is overblown and the related paragraph is full of fluff. Thus, it is when the client is authentic that he can be of the best help to you.

Related Terms/Phrases:
Attestation
Commendation
Endorsement
Positive Review

First Appearance: Ninth sentence in the twentieth paragraph of the Renewal Letter. The Renewal Letter opens with, "Having a Life Coaching business...." The twentieth paragraph begins, "Or maybe you want...." The ninth sentence starts, "Or even how to ask a client...." (p. 43)

## Theory

Definition – A group of proposed ideas or an empirically supported selection of opinions that purport to explain a phenomenon or that delineate an approach to a task, problem, or situation

Further Thoughts: In Life Coaching, there is not a selection of standard theoretical orientations that students are required to learn about, choose from, and then master in order to obtain a degree so as to later qualify for licensure, not like with psychology. Still, coaching does have roots in the philosophies of Positive Psychology. The short of this is that coaching looks to identify and capitalize on a client's strengths and move that client beyond surviving to something more.

Your role as the coach is to formulate your own theory about how to practice Life Coaching well and to adhere to it. Your theory is more of a personalized approach, but if you choose to formally educate yourself, you may learn about structured methods such as Cognitive Behavioral Coaching and learn from them. You may, if you decide, even crystallize your approach into a true theory and do research into it and refine it until it is empirically supported. How far you go with this is up to you. What you must do is share with the client the basic philosophies of Life Coaching and work from coaching's four pillars – listening, asking powerful questions, creating accountability, and designing action plans.

The client's role in relationship to theory is to be informed about the process of coaching and to use what is offered and available to better her own life. Again, she does not need to be a scholar in theory, only understand how the primary tenets of coaching work so she can collaborate with you to create the Thinking Space. Understanding what is expected of her as the client and how to meet those expectations by putting forth effort and being accountable is essential.

Related Terms/Phrases:
Approach
Ideology
Method
Orientation
Philosophy
System

First Appearance: First sentence in the seventh paragraph of the Renewal Letter. The Renewal Letter opens with, "Having a Life Coaching business...." The seventh paragraph begins, "Perhaps a theory...." The first sentence is the beginning of the seventh paragraph and thus has the same start as the paragraph itself. (p. 41)

## Therapy

Definition – An approach to mental health treatment that focuses on helping a client return to an average or baseline level of functioning

Further Thoughts: In Life Coaching, clients that are in therapy are generally not appropriate for coaching. On occasion, there are can be exceptions. It is always important for the client to talk with his therapist in order to make sure the therapist agrees that Life Coaching can proceed without impeding the therapeutic process.

Your role as a coach in regard to therapy is to make sure any prospective clients understand the difference between Life Coaching services and therapy services. In addition, it is important that you make a referral for any clients that exhibit signs of a mental health issue. In the event that you have established a connection with a network of professionals that include the names of specific therapists who have good reputations in the community, you might offer a specific name or two. If not, you might wish to mention that it might be helpful for the client to rule out the need for psychological services and suggest he get in contact with his insurance company to find the name of a professional in the local area. Beyond making a referral and either not starting, pausing, or discontinuing services based on the need of client or the prospective client who is dealing with a mental health issue, you do not have further responsibilities in terms of therapy.

The client's role in therapy, as regards its relationship to coaching, is to be clear that coaching is a different sort of service. In the event that he has been given a referral by you, it is his job to follow through on seeking en evaluation to determine if he needs further professional help. By making this referral, you are performing a service for the client, an important one, one that is within your realm of competence.

Related Terms/Phrases:
Mental Health Treatment
The Talking Cure

First Appearance: Second sentence in the eleventh paragraph of Contemplation Letter 2. Contemplation Letter 2 opens with, "Your mind may be filled with thoughts…." The eleventh paragraph begins, "If consulting is what calls to you…." The second sentence starts, "If therapy is what speaks to you…." (p. 7)

## Thinking Space™

Definition – The time and space created by a Life Coach for a Life Coaching client, with collaboration from the client, in which the coaching conversation takes place

Further Thoughts: In Life Coaching, all conversations take place within the Thinking Space. The Thinking Space is created from the coach's belief in the client and results from the interest paid to the client by the coach. In order to be a true Thinking Space, the coach must be patient and approach listening, asking powerful questions, creating accountability, and designing action plans with ease. By modeling a quiet confidence and communicating to the client, often through action rather than words, that she can take her time in designing and building her dreamed of and sought after life, the coach helps the client appreciate the journey as well as the destination. Thus, as the coach, you are responsible for creating the Thinking Space and for maintaining it.

The client, in turn, helps you create the Thinking Space by being an active participant in the coaching process. She shares, listens, asks questions, cocreates accountability, and co-designs action plans. She identifies what she wants to work toward and puts the necessary time and energy into achieving her dreams.

Related Terms/Phrases:
Coaching Call
Coaching Conversation
Coaching Environment
Coaching Office

First Appearance: Third sentence in the sixth paragraph of Contemplation Letter 3. Contemplation Letter 3 opens with, "At this stage, you may be wondering…." The sixth paragraph begins, "Every Life Coaching conversation includes…." The third sentence starts, "This is often one of the most enticing…." (p. 9)

## Thought

Definition – An idea or notion

Further Thoughts: In Life Coaching, thoughts are the focus of conversation. Life Coaching exists to help the client improve the quality of his thoughts, which, in turn, improves the quality of his life.

Your role as the coach is to support the client in the pursuit of his dreams so he can move from surviving to thriving. You can do this by engaging with the coaching process – through listening, asking powerful questions, creating accountability, and designing action plans. The goal is to have the client be able to function as his own support outside of the session. Over time, he will learn to better listen to himself, to ask of himself questions that are thought-provoking and that help him create a path to travel, so he can achieve what he wants most to achieve.

The client's role is to get back in touch with himself, to maintain contact with his core self, to listen to what he thinks and feels, and to expand upon the dialogue he has with himself so that he can determine what his values are, what is most important for him to pursue. He can do this by participating in the coaching process, by collaborating with you the coach to create the Thinking Space. He must hold himself accountable, work toward his goals, choose what to focus on in between sessions, and fulfill his commitments. By being an active thinker and an active listener to himself, the client can transform himself and his life.

Related Terms/Phrases:
Belief
Idea
Notion
Reflection

First Appearance: In plural form. Second sentence in the third paragraph of the Pre-Contemplation Letter. The Pre-Contemplation Letter opens with, "You might be wondering why...." The third paragraph begins, "So, treat yourself for making it this far...." The second sentence starts, "And, if you'd like, you can explore...." (p. 4)

## Thriving

Definition – To be living from an inspired place that takes into account one's values and wants and that results in joy, fulfillment, and self-actualization

Further Thoughts: In Life Coaching, the goal of living is to thrive. The client comes to the process not to get by, not to do okay, but to move beyond existing and surviving.

Your role as the coach is to the help the client ascertain what is most important to her, often by helping her identify and work from her values. Once she knows these whys – the reasons behind her goals and dreams – she can move toward creating a pathway to achieving all that she wants to achieve. The support you provide comes from listening, asking thought-provoking, powerful questions, creating accountability, and designing action plans. You and the client work hand in hand to form and then engage with each other in the Thinking Space.

The client's role is to define what thriving means to her, to create an individualized formula for joy and success that has the heart of who she is and where she wants to go at its core. Then, from there, she can apply the effort and do the work necessary to turn her personalized dreams and wishes into reality.

Related Terms/Phrases:
Be the Best You Can Be
Do Well
Flourish
Live With Purpose
Self-Actualize
Succeed

First Appearance: Fourth sentence in the first paragraph of Contemplation Letter 3. Contemplation Letter 3 opens with, "At this stage, you may be wondering…." The first paragraph is the beginning of the letter and thus has the same beginning as the letter itself. The fourth sentence starts, "Anyone who wants to move beyond…." (p. 9)

## Time

Definition – A measured period during which an event or action takes place or during which a condition exists, often denoted in seconds, minutes, hours, days, weeks, months, and years; also, the relationship between moments or between an individual and such moments, often denoted as past, present, and future

Further Thoughts: In Life Coaching, time carries many distinctions. Life Coaching is aimed at improving the future by working and making progress in the present. The past is only occasionally checked in with when necessary, often during discussions of strengths or successes that can be brought forward or during review of core beliefs and their relationship to childhood conclusions.

Your role as the coach is to make sure time is an asset not a liability. Specifically, the client may regret that he has not accomplished certain things yet or he may wish to make every dream come true in an unreasonable time frame. It is your job to help the client focus on the present rather than the past and assist the client in creating achievable goals. Again, you will rely on the basics of the coaching process – listening, asking powerful questions, creating accountability, and designing action plans – to make this happen.

The client's role is to learn to see time as a construct upon which value, often via societal expectations, is placed. Thus, the client may come to the process with a list of shoulds – things he believes he has to do – based on his age and stage of life. He must then challenge these shoulds by exploring what he truly wants based on his values and what is important to him. By replacing ought tos with want tos, the client is well positioned to make use of his present in order to build his dreamed of future.

Related Terms/Phrases:
Duration
Length
Span

First Appearance: First sentence in the ninth paragraph of Contemplation Letter 1. Contemplation Letter 1 opens with, "Your journey to becoming a Life Coach…." The ninth paragraph begins, "No matter where the idea of Life Coaching…." The first sentence is the beginning of the ninth paragraph and thus has the same start as the paragraph itself. (p. 5)

## Time Management

Definition – The method by which a person schedules and completes tasks and activities

Further Thoughts: In Life Coaching, good time management is essential. Difficulties with time management and organization are often stumbling blocks for the client and may have previously hampered her ability to achieve.

Your role as the coach is to help the client appropriately manage her time. This is best addressed through accountability measures and action plans. If you choose to use the S.M.A.R.T. goals formula, then time is taken into account. Use of this system means that goals must be well-defined and have concrete criteria that mark them as complete. They must be assigned a time frame that is realistic and allows for completion of the necessary steps.

By checking in with the client during each session about her progress, any challenges she met along the way as well as how to address them, and by helping her decide what to devote her energy to next, you are supporting her in her commitment to her goals. You are helping make sure time does not slip away from her.

The client's role in relationship to time management is to learn to balance her responsibilities so that adequate time can be devoted to the goals she is working on in Life Coaching. If she has difficulty getting something done during the time she has allotted for herself, it is important that she bring that up with you and work toward correcting what needs to be corrected. The client who tends to overschedule herself will have to learn to be more realistic about what can be accomplished during a 24-hour time period. The client who underschedules herself will have to learn how to build and sustain momentum so that she can achieve that which she wants to achieve.

Related Terms/Phrases:
Appointing Time
Reserving Time
Scheduling

First Appearance: Third sentence in the seventh paragraph of Action Letter 2. Action Letter 2 opens with, "Now that you have decided…." The seventh paragraph begins, "What does this mean about time…." The third sentence starts, "Will you have to focus more closely…." (p. 26)

## Timing

Definition – An occurrence of an event, action, process, or condition, which is often viewed as either conducive to success or sustainment or not; also, the ability to decide when to do something that creates an optimal outcome

Further Thoughts: In Life Coaching, timing is important. The client comes to the process when he is ready to work toward thriving. Thus, it is important, as the coach, that you build upon this momentum.

Your role is to engage the client with the process and set him up on a road to success at the outset. At first, success can be measured by his participation in the coaching conversation and his collaborative creation of the Thinking Space. Later, success can be measured by the client's better understanding of and ability to commune with himself – his thoughts, feelings, approaches to life, values, wants, and dreams. Then, success in Life Coaching becomes about the progress he has made toward his goals and his appreciation for his own journey.

The client's role in timing is to utilize his skills in this area if he already has them or to develop them if he doesn't. He must use timing to increase his outcomes. He must decide upon the order of steps, understanding which will work better where. Timing is a skill that often improves over time. Thus, the client will likely get better with timing by doing and learning from its related outcomes.

Related Terms/Phrases:
Deadline
Schedule
Set Up

First Appearance: Fourth sentence in the seventh paragraph of Action Letter 2. Action Letter 2 opens with, "Now that you have decided...." The seventh paragraph begins, "What does this mean about time...." The fourth sentence starts, "And the timing...." (p. 26)

## Tolerate

Definition – To allow without protest; to put up with or endure

Further Thoughts: In Life Coaching, the client often comes to the process with a litany of things she is tolerating in her life. Part of the coaching process is to have the client eliminate those things that drain her time and energy so that she can make room for the things that contribute to her vitality and well-being.

Your role as the coach is to help the client determine what things she is tolerating, those items, processes, or people she has allowed to stay in her life, but which are not contributing to it in a positive way. Then, once this is done, your job is to support her as she makes any desired changes. You may utilize a particular exercise to do this and devote a session or two to getting the process started or the gains made in this area may occur as a natural result of other endeavors.

The client's role is to identify the people, places, things, and processes that contribute to her life and those that do not. Then, she must decide what, if any, changes she would like to make in order to recapture time and energy so she may devote them to the betterment of her life and the advancement of her dreams. In the event that this process is one the client elects to have occur naturally, the removal of tolerations often occurs as they are identified as stumbling blocks to her goals.

Related Terms/Phrases:
Abide
Allow
Endure
Permit
Wait Out

First Appearance: Fifth sentence in the ninth paragraph of Action Letter 4. Action Letter 4 opens with, "You are graduating from training…." The ninth paragraph begins, "Would a visualization…." The fifth sentence starts, "A day that is free…." (p. 30)

## Tool

Definition – Something that is necessary to or assists in the completion of a task or the ongoing nature of a process

Further Thoughts: In Life Coaching, tools are identified and put to use. The client often brings to coaching a set of tools and skills that can immediately be incorporated into discussion and planning. Through the creation of goals and the work done to accomplish dreams, it is common for a gap in skills or the absence of a tool to be uncovered. This is a standard part of the process and is an opportunity for the client to improve either himself or his access to resources.

Your role as the coach is to help the client identify what tools he already has at his disposal and which ones he needs to develop in order to make his dreams come true. By closely examining stumbling blocks, hesitations the client has in moving forward, and moments when the client feels stuck, the absence of tools or the belief that a tool is not present is determined. Some solutions involve substituting a skill that is not in the client's possession with one that is. Others involve further learning or practice so that a latent ability is developed into a usable talent. Still others involve recognizing what is already there, but has existed outside of the client's awareness.

The client's role in regard to tools is to be willing to explore, use, and add to the skills in his possession. By being amenable to growth and matching the right process with the right approach, the client significantly enhances the breadth, depth, and expediency of his success.

Related Terms/Phrases:
Approach
Resource
Skill
Strategy

First Appearance: In plural form. Fourth sentence in the eighth paragraph of Contemplation Letter 2. Contemplation Letter 2 opens with, ""Your mind may be filled with…." The eighth paragraph begins, "Are you ready to delve…." The fourth sentence starts, "To provide tools for replacing…." (p. 7)

## Transformation

Definition – The act or process of changing, often in a positive direction

Further Thoughts: In Life Coaching, positive transformation is the goal. The client comes to the process in order to evolve into the person she wants to be so she can live the life she wants to live.

Your role as the coach is to help the client make the changes to herself and her life that she seeks. A significant portion of this will involve her recognizing previous successes and building upon them in order to create future successes. Deep listening is one of the most transformative tools you have at your disposal as a coach. Along with asking powerful questions, deep listening allows you to help the client learn to think, feel, and behave in ways that close the gap between where she is and where she wants to be.

The client's role in transformation is to identify what she wants to change and work toward such changes. Meaningful transformation must include an appreciation for what has already been accomplished. It must also include a deep appreciation for self. By recognizing her uniqueness, engaging with her talents, and putting her values at the center of her life, the client transforms her relationship with her life and herself in a way that allows her to feel complete and fulfilled.

Related Terms/Phrases:
Development
Evolution
Self-Actualization
Transcendence

First Appearance: Fourth sentence in the seventh paragraph of Contemplation Letter 5. Contemplation Letter 5 opens with, "It's good to see you...." The seventh paragraph begins, "Another option is the certificate...." The fourth sentence starts, "From personal transformation to...." (p. 13)

## Transition

Definition – A move from one place, subject, state, or phase to another; also, the act or process of such a move

Further Thoughts: In Life Coaching, the client will be transitioning. He will be moving from where he is to where he wants to be. He will also be moving from who he is to who he wants to be.

Your role as the coach is to support this process. By helping him clarify what he wants to keep in his life and what he wants to let go, you can assist him in choosing what is most important to him. Then, from there, an approach to getting what he wants can be developed. Goals can be assigned timelines. And the work that needs to be done can be done.

The client's role is to be clear about the direction in which he wants to go. By exploring his values and identifying what is most important to him, he can ensure that forward movement is actually true progress not just a step in a meaningless direction. By recognizing the importance of his journey, he can engage with each step along the way, thereby being a part of the entire transition process he is undertaking. This will allow him to replicate successful change in the future if he so wishes.

Related Terms/Phrases:
Change
Evolution
Growth
Move
Shift
Transformation

First Appearance: Second sentence in the seventh paragraph of Contemplation Letter 4. Contemplation Letter 4 opens with, "It's at this stage...." The seventh paragraph begins, "For those interested in general self-improvement...." The second sentence starts, "For those facing a transition...." (p. 11)

## Unconscious

Definition – The part of the mind that exists outside of a person's awareness.

Further Thoughts: In Life Coaching, expansion of awareness and, therefore, a client's conscious mind is part of the process. The term, unconscious mind, comes from Freud who first made the distinction between the information and mental processes outside of a person's awareness and those within. The opposite of the unconscious mind is the conscious mind.

Your role as the coach is to help a client access the thoughts and ideas in her unconscious mind. Unlike with therapy, you will not go rooting around in her thoughts via clinical methods. Rather, you will help create opportunities for the client to get know herself, especially through the identification of her wants and values. You will also help her access what she does know by taking the time to examine her experiences, especially her successes.

The role of the client is to be open to the process of learning about herself. As such, she will learn just how much she thinks and knows, about herself, others, and the world, even if that information is far from her everyday thoughts. Over time, she will develop methods to increase the speed with which she can bring information from her mental depths to the surface.

Related Terms/Phrases:
Beneath One's Awareness
Outside of One's Awareness
Unconscious Mind

First Appearance: Fifth sentence in the eighth paragraph of Contemplation Letter 2. Contemplation Letter 2 opens with, ""Your mind may be filled with…." The eighth paragraph begins, "Are you ready to delve…." The fifth sentence starts, "To deeply explore…." (p. 7)

## Value

Definition – Relative worth or importance of a person, place, thing, idea, situation, or process

Further Thoughts: In Life Coaching, values are behind what the client chooses to work on. Whether or not those values are explicitly implored or the client selects topics and goals that feel important in some way, values bring meaning to the client's life.

Your role as the coach is to offer the client the opportunity to do values work if he is interested. This can be as unstructured as asking him to tell you what is most important to him or as structured as using a focused approach, such as Values Processing Coaching, to assist the client in identifying and working from his values. By listening, asking powerful questions, creating accountability, and designing action plans, you can support the client in living life from his values.

The client's role is to be aware of his values and work from them if he so chooses. Happiness is said to result from being satisfied with what one has. One of the best methods for achieving this type of satisfaction is to pursue what is important in the first place. The client can undertake this journey towards meaning and joy by using his values to inspire his goals and dreams.

Related Terms/Phrases:
Guiding Principle
Object of Significance
Treasured Person

First Appearance: First sentence in the twelfth paragraph of Contemplation Letter 5. Contemplation Letter 5 opens with, "It's good to see you...." The twelfth paragraph begins, "Perhaps there is a certain personal value...." The first sentence is the beginning of the twelfth paragraph and thus has the same start as the paragraph itself. (p. 14)

## Vision

Definition – A picture of the future or an imagined result of an idea, feeling, situation, course of action, or process

Further Thoughts: In Life Coaching, a vision of the future is a powerful thing. It can be purposefully invoked via a technique to help the client determine what she truly wants or it can result naturally from the coaching conversation and serve as a snapshot of something for her to strive for.

Your role as the coach is to assist the client in creating a picture of the future that is motivating and helps guide the client forward. Again, formal exercises can be used to draw the client's vision forth or attention can be paid to regular coaching conversations to help the client catch when she is painting a picture of her wants and dreams.

The client's role in regard to vision is to be open to using her sense of sight, and related ability to imagine a picture, to assist her in sketching out the particularities of her dreams. Using vision as a tool often informs the coaching process and allows for the creation of concrete goals that are in line with the client's most fundamental imaginings. Checking in with her vision, including noting the ways in which it has changed, can be a helpful tool to understanding exactly what the clients wants to come to pass. In this way, satisfaction with accomplishments is increased and joy is more likely to result from any and all accomplishments made.

Related Terms/Phrases:
Concept
Dream
Idea
Imagining
Mental Image
Picture
Visualization

First Appearance: Seventh sentence in the sixth paragraph of Contemplation Letter 1. Contemplation Letter 1 opens with, "Your journey to becoming a Life Coach…." The sixth paragraph begins, "Why has your mind suggested…." The seventh sentence starts, "Or is the why a vision…." (p. 5)

## Visualization

Definition – Formation of a pictured scenario, situation, or result

Further Thoughts: In Life Coaching, visualizations often come in the form of exercises. One of the most common visualization exercises is the Perfect Day scenario. With this technique, the client imagines his perfect day and either discusses or writes down the details of that, beginning from the time he gets up to the time he goes to sleep. He documents the whos, whats, wheres, whys, whens, and hows of his day. The information from the exercise is then used to help the client construct his ideal future.

Often, it is helpful to have the client imagine a perfect workday as well as a perfect weekend day or vacation day since these types of days are likely to be significantly different from each other. Variants of this exercise abound and can be used to create a perfect image of any scenario from a date to a business meeting to a party.

Your role as the coach is to help the client picture his ideal future. Whether this is through basic listening and the asking of questions or the result of an intricate coaching exercise depends upon your preferred approach and the needs and wants of the client.

The client's role in this process is to be clear about how he sees his future and what he wants from it. He must then create goals that help him get there. It is important that he remain appreciative of his efforts and aware of the importance of his journey. Often, if the client participates in visualization exercises, elements of his values will insert themselves into his imaginings, thereby helping him move toward a more satisfying path in life.

Related Terms/Phrases:
Dream
Imagination Exercise
Mental Image
Vision
Visualization Exercise
Visualization Technique

First Appearance: First sentence in the ninth paragraph of Action Letter 4. Action Letter 4 opens with, "You are graduating from training…." The ninth paragraph begins, "Would a visualization…." The first sentence is the beginning of the ninth paragraph and thus has the same start as the paragraph itself. (p. 30)

## Want

Definition – A desire; also, the object of desire

Further Thoughts: In Life Coaching, wants take center stage in terms of goals and action plans. Needs and requirements are not the only considerations at play. Your role as the coach is to help the client draw out her wants so that she is aware of the things she would most like to strive for. This may take some getting used to for the client as many children receive a strong message about the importance of needs in childhood; wants, in contrast, are identified as optional.

Of course, wants are optional in terms of survival. In terms of thriving, however, they are indispensable. Thus, it is important that the client understand, if self-actualization is the aim and joy the hallmark of its achievement, wants must be met in some capacity.

The client's role in regard to wants is to decide what hers are and to delineate ways she can fulfill them. Whether this takes the form of having more down time for herself or increasing her exposure to things that bring her satisfaction, such as trips to museums or time with friends, it is important that she understand those things she would like to incorporate into her life, the things that make her life more meaningful to her, that transform living from a task to a dream.

Related Terms/Phrases:
Aspiration
Desire
Dream
Fancy
Longing
Wish

First Appearance: Third sentence in the third paragraph of the Intro-duction Letter. The Introduction Letter opens with, "Somehow this book has found its way...." The third paragraph begins, "What follows are a series of letters...." The third sentence starts, ""For those recently started on the journey...." (p. 3)

## Weakness

Definition – An area of diminished competence, either in comparison to one's own abilities or in comparison to the abilities of others in the same area

Further Thoughts: In Life Coaching, weaknesses are seen as challenges or opportunities. They often go by different names as well, including growth opportunity, growth point, point of improvement, etc.

Your role as the coach is to help the client view weaknesses in a positive light, as opportunities for the expansion of himself or his life or as challenges that he can meet with a little applied attention and effort. Weaknesses often reveal themselves as the cause of stumbling blocks or in moments when the client feels stuck or hesitant to proceed. In these cases, it will be your job to assist the client in identifying the issue at hand and creating a way to address it that is effective and helps diminish the likelihood of its reoccurrence in the future.

The client's role in regard to weaknesses is to be willing to work through challenges and stumbling blocks, including accepting them as a natural part of life and of the coaching process. By reframing them in this way, and accepting them as a necessary part of success and progress, he can position himself to benefit from them rather than be paralyzed by them.

Related Terms/Phrases:
Challenge
Deficiency
Flaw
Growth Opportunity
Shortcoming

First Appearance: In plural form. Third sentence in the eighth paragraph of Contemplation Letter 2. Contemplation Letter 2 opens with, "Your mind may be filled with…." The eighth paragraph begins, "Are you ready to delve…." The third sentence starts, "To explore strengths…." (p. 7)

## Welcome Packet

Definition – A collection of forms given to the client, prior to the first session, to read, fill out, and/or sign whose purpose is to introduce the client to the coaching process, document the client's consent to coaching parameters, and facilitate the client's ability to provide pertinent information to the coach

Further Thoughts: In Life Coaching, the Welcome Packet is a common tool. The Welcome Packet typically includes a Coaching Agreement, which delineates the coach's and client's responsibilities; a Consent to Coaching form, which describes the limits of confidentiality and the fact that privilege is not a legal right in coaching; an Intake Questionnaire, which gathers demographic and pertinent background information about the client as well as information about what the client would like to work on; and the Life Wheel, which assesses the client's satisfaction with a selection of life areas.

Your role as the coach is to have such paperwork available and accessible to the client. It is important that, at the very least, you make sure the client's consent to coaching is documented in written form. It is also advisable that the client be issued a written version of her responsibilities and your responsibilities as a coach. The actual intake procedure and the review of the Life Wheel, if you choose to use it, can be done verbally, if you wish.

The client's role in the process is to complete any necessary paperwork and to make sure she understands the information being provided to her. Though the client might want to gloss over limits of confidentiality and your expectation of her responsibilities, it is important that you and she are clear about the parameters of the coaching relationship. Being clear often prevents misunderstandings and sticky situations in the future.

Related Terms/Phrases:
Intake Packet
New Client Packet

First Appearance: In plural form. Fifth sentence in the fifth paragraph of Action Letter 6. Action Letter 6 opens with, "By now, you have set a few goals…." The fifth paragraph begins, "Have you already identified people…." The fifth sentence starts, "Will you be comparing welcome packets…." (p. 34)

## What

Definition – The object or goal of coaching; also, the resources necessary for a process or course of action

Further Thoughts: In Life Coaching, whats are important. They describe the goals the client has, the things the client would like to achieve. They also describe the resources necessary for such achievement.

Your role as the coach is discuss with the client his wants so you have a clear picture of those ends you are trying to help the client meet or reach. The coaching conversation is the primary vehicle for exploring wants and planning for their attainment. Assessments and exercises may be used to further delineate wants or to help the client flesh out a path for getting to where he wishes to go.

The client's role is to make sure he is clear about the things he wishes to obtain and the successes he wishes to achieve. If he is willing, participating in values work, which reveals the whys of coaching, can help him better understand and construct his wants. Regardless, it is the client's responsibility to name what he and you are playing for as part of the coaching process.

Related Terms/Phrases:
Desire
End
Goal
Measure of Success
Object
Want

First Appearance: In plural form. Second sentence in the fourth paragraph of Contemplation Letter 1. Contemplation Letter 1 opens with, "Your journey to becoming a Life Coach began...." The fourth paragraph begins, "There are many questions you can ask..." The second sentence in the paragraph starts, "Some of those questions deal with..." (p. 5)

# When

Definition – At what time; during which time

Further Thoughts: In Life Coaching, whens are primarily attached to goals and deadlines. Work is done in the present and is for the purpose of building a better future.

Your role as the coach is to assist the client in assigning time frames and deadlines for her goals. These time frames will vary. Some will be aimed at completion in the near future; these are called short-term deadlines. Others will extend out months, a year, or several years; these are called long-term deadlines.

The client's role in terms of when is to share her preference for the attainment of dreams and completion of goals. She often has an order in her mind for approaching her wants. If not, she may wish to explore whens in order to create an order. Only by having a clear idea of the timing of goals and the expected attainment of dreams can the client and you be on the same page.

Whens also come about in deciding the timing of sessions. Scheduling dates and times for coaching sessions is a shared responsibility between you and the client.

Related Terms/Phrases:
Deadline
Target Date
Time Frame
Time Limit

First Appearance: In plural form. Fourth sentence in the fourth paragraph of Contemplation Letter 1. Contemplation Letter 1 opens with, "Your journey to becoming a Life Coach began...." The fourth paragraph begins, "There are many questions you can ask..." The fourth sentence in the paragraph starts, "Whens, wheres, and whos...." (p. 5)

## Where

Definition – To, in, or at what place; also, to, in, or at what direction, position, or situation

Further Thoughts: In Life Coaching, where is a covered topic. Though wheres are not at the forefront of discussion in the same way that whats, whys, and hows are, wheres designate the place goals will take place or dreams will come to fruition.

Your role as the coach is to address wheres as needed. For example, the client might need to explore options for where he can open a business or have a meeting or go for exercise. Wheres typically come up when goals are being operationalized and action plans designed.

The client's role is to be clear about wheres when to be clear is necessary. Again, the client may have to make choices about wheres as part of fleshing out his goals and creating accountability measures.

Wheres also come about in deciding the place or related method by which the client and you will have a coaching conversation. You might meet with the client in your office or you might be in two different places and have a session via phone or video. You and the client can work together to decide the environment that works best from among those options offered by you.

Related Terms/Phrases:
Location
Place
Setting

First Appearance: In plural form. Fourth sentence in the fourth paragraph of Contemplation Letter 1. Contemplation Letter 1 opens with, "Your journey to becoming a Life Coach began...." The fourth paragraph begins, "There are many questions you can ask..." The fourth sentence in the paragraph starts, "Whens, wheres, and whos...." (p. 5)

## Who

Definition – The person or people involved

Further Thoughts: In Life Coaching, whos are a part of the coaching discussion. The who of the coaching conversation is the client and you, the coach. The whos that relate to the client's goals and dreams are up to the client.

Your role as the coach in regard to whos is to determine who might be supporting the client's goals, either as a member of the client's support network or as a part of the dream-to-reality-making process. If the client chooses to delegate certain responsibilities, it is helpful for you to know a name or company title you can refer to in order to ask about progress. Even if the client is not completing a certain piece of the overall picture, the completion of that piece may still affect the client's ability to move forward with her own responsibilities. Thus, being able to reference pertinent whos can help in the creation of accountability and the design of action plans.

The client's role is to decide who she wants to know about her goals and dreams, who she will rely on for support, and who she may incorporate into the process. The coaching conversation can often help her solidify her tentative plans or help her see where a who is missing in the process.

Related Terms/Phrases:
Business
Company
Individual
Individuals
Person
People

First Appearance: In plural form. Fourth sentence in the fourth paragraph of Contemplation Letter 1. Contemplation Letter 1 opens with, "Your journey to becoming a Life Coach began...." The fourth paragraph begins, "There are many questions you can ask..." The fourth sentence in the paragraph starts, "Whens, wheres, and whos...." (p. 5)

## Why

Definition – The cause, purpose, reason, or value behind an action, dream, goal, or process

Further Thoughts: In Life Coaching, whys are an essential part of the process. When a client understands the whys behinds his whats, he is better equipped to reach his dreams. Whys, which often take the form of values, bring with them satisfaction and meaning.

Your role as the coach is to help the client identify the whys that are the driving force of his whats. Values work is one way whys can be addressed. In the event that the client is not interested in doing formal values work, engagement in the coaching process can help delineate at least some reasons for the client's chosen goals.

The client's role in regard to whys is to identify what his are and to come up with goals that help him work towards those things that bring him satisfaction and meaning. The client is the only one who can identify his whys. True understanding of whys requires and facilitates true understanding of self. Thus, the most intimate relationship a client can have with himself depends upon his familiarity with the whys that guide him and his life.

Related Terms/Phrases:
Aim
Aspiration
Catalyst
Draw
Inspiration
Motivation
Rationale
Reason

First Appearance: In plural form. Fifth sentence in the fourth paragraph of Contemplation Letter 1. Contemplation Letter 1 opens with, "Your journey to becoming a Life Coach began...." The fourth paragraph begins, "There are many questions you can ask..." The fifth sentence in the paragraph starts, "And Life Coaching, masterful Life Coaching...." (p. 5)

## Wisdom

Definition – Knowledge or insight that results from experience or an innate understanding of oneself, others, and the world, especially in terms of thoughts and thinking patterns, feelings and feeling patterns, behaviors and behavioral patterns, situations and situational patterns, and/or processes and patterns of process

Further Thoughts: In Life Coaching, wisdom is brought to the process and results from the process. The client is the person that knows herself the best. She has been with herself the longest and has experienced her thinking, feeling, and behaving as well as the results of her thinking, feeling, and behavior patterns the most.

Your role as the coach is to help the client access her own wisdom so she can use the related kernels of insight and truth to help her reach her coaching goals. Listening and asking powerful questioning are often the most helpful in identifying and growing a client's wisdom.

The client's role is to access her own wisdom and apply it to her coaching goals. By mining past experiences of success and sharing what she knows about her herself, her life, and her dreams, she is well positioned to use her insight into herself, others, and the world to build the life she wants to live and be the person she dreams of being.

Related Terms/Phrases:
Awareness
Experience
Foresight
Insight
Judgment
Knowledge
Savvy

First Appearance: First sentence in the seventeenth paragraph of Determination Letter 1. Determination Letter 1 opens with, "Now is the tricky part..." The seventeenth paragraph begins, "Together, your mind and heart...." The first sentence is the beginning of the seventeenth paragraph and thus has the same start as the paragraph itself. (p. 20)

# ACKNOWLEDGEMENTS

## Inspiration

This book is an extension of the project I was required to complete in order to receive my Master Certified Life Coaching (MCLC) certificate. It was the first idea I had when I discovered I needed to create original content to contribute to the field of Life Coaching. It was also the project that spoke most deeply to me and still does today.

## Title

The title of this book is a play on Rainier Maria Rilke's book, *Letters to a Young Poet*.

## Structure

The use of letters and the inclusion of notes related to those letters are inspired by *Letters to a Young Poet* as well. The original text did not incorporate definitions; instead, it provided both historical and personal contexts related to what Rilke was sharing with the poet to whom he was writing. I thoroughly recommend *Letters to a Young Poet* to anyone and everyone as the themes found in it relate to living life, not just writing poetry.

Though the organization of letters around stages of change is my original concept, the stages of change used are those found in the Transtheoretical Model of Change created in the 1990s by Dr. James O. Prochaska and Dr. Carlo Di Clemente. I cannot name the exact book in which I first encountered this model. However, I can say it was part of my psychology training at the Florida Institute of Technology (FIT). Whether it was self-assigned reading or a formal requirement, I cannot recall. A few of the terms vary across different presentations of the model. I chose to use the term Determination instead of the more popular term Preparation for the third stage of change because I thought it better fit with the tone of the letters found in that related section. From addiction and recovery treatment paradigms, I brought in the idea of a stage that follows Maintenance. In alcohol and drug treatment that phase is referred to as a Relapse. It may also be called Slip. Since that exact concept does not apply, but the need to get back in touch with foundations and basics does, I named my stage Renewal. I also placed it prior to Maintenance as I see it as occurring for the first time earlier than long-term maintenance. I also chose not to reference the Termination stage of change as I do not believe anyone ever stops being a Life Coach. Coaches only stop providing professional services. Thus, my final letter relates to a stage I created called Legacy, which is based on Erik Erikson's psychosocial stage, Generativity vs. Stagnation, and can be found in his Theory of Psychosocial Development.

## General

I completed my Life Coach training at the American School of Professional Life Coaching (ASPLC). Therefore, I owe the director of the school, Dr. Elliot B. Rosenbaum, a special acknowledgment as he introduced me to many of the resources listed below. In addition, a significant portion of the new Life Coaching terms included in this book I first encountered either in mentoring sessions with him or training sessions he conducted. I will highlight the most novel ones throughout these acknowledgements.

I also owe a special acknowledgement to Dr. Patrick Williams. His books comprised a large portion of the foundational texts I read when I was starting out in Life Coaching. His lectures also introduced me to several coaching specific terms that are found across the literature.

And I owe a special acknowledgement to the professors at the Florida Institute of Technology (FIT), also known as Florida Tech. I received both my Master of Science (M.S.) in Psychology and Doctorate of Psychology (Psy.D.) degrees from the university. My training as a psychologist heavily informs my approach to Life Coaching even though I recognize and profess that Life Coaching services are significantly different from therapy services.

# THE LETTERS

## Introduction Letter

The term beginner's mind I first encountered in Dr. Patrick Williams' and Dr. Diane Menendez's book, *Becoming a Professional Life Coach: Lessons from the Institute of Life Coach Training, 2nd Edition*.

## Pre-Contemplation Letter

The frequent reference to thoughts, feelings, and behaviors, which are part of the thought-feeling-behavior triad of human behavior, comes from my training in Cognitive-Behavioral Therapy (CBT). CBT was created and pioneered by Dr. Aaron T. Beck in the 1960s. He and his daughter, Dr. Judith S. Beck, have written numerous books on the subject. In fact, one of the most popular books on the subject was written by Dr. Judith Beck: *Cognitive Behavior Therapy: Basics and Beyond*, which is now in its second edition. Dr. Beck's book is the first one I read on CBT.

I first encountered the term Cognitive Behavioral Coaching (CBC) during a mentoring session with Dr. Rosenbaum. This theoretical orientation best represents my approach to Life Coaching. Also, its use of thoughts, feelings, and behaviors to help promote client achievement heavily influences the writings in this book.

The term appreciation in so far as how it is used in coaching I also first encountered during mentoring sessions with Dr. Rosenbaum.

## Contemplation Letter # 1

The focus on whats, hows, and whys comes from the framework Dr. Rosenbaum uses to explain both the beginning, middle, and end of the coaching session as well as the beginning, middle, and end of the coaching relationship. Whys, especially, are a focus of his work. His book, *The Valued Self: Five Steps to Healthy Self-Esteem*, outlines an approach to the exploration of whys called Values Processing Therapy (VPT), which includes identification of values and living life based on them. His follow up, *The Essential Self: The Key to a Life of Passion, Lasting Joy, and Fulfillment*, continues his work with values and their relationship to a person's core. *The Valued Self* and *The Essential Self* are two of my favorite psychology and coaching texts to date.

The term act of life is also one I first encountered during a mentoring session with Dr. Rosenbaum. In the framework discussed, there are three acts of life. I have taken poetic license with this term, using it in its original form as well as expanding upon it for illustrative purposes.

## Contemplation Letter # 2

The distinctions between being a therapist, consultant, and coach I first encountered during my mentoring sessions with Dr. Rosenbaum. I further read about these topics in Dr. Patrick Williams' and Dr. Diane Menendez's book, *Becoming a Professional Life Coach: Lessons from the Institute of Life Coach Training, 2nd Edition*, and Dr. Patrick Williams' and Dr. Deborah C. Davis' book, *Therapist as Life Coach: An Introduction for Counselors and Other Helping Professionals, Revised and Expanded*. The distinctions included in this book are informed by my learning and include my own take and thoughts.

The terms conscious and unsconscious mind come form the teachings of Sigmund Freud. Again, I cannot say the exact book I first encountered these terms in. However, they are discussed in many of Freud's writings. His book, *The Ego and The Id*, is probably a good place to start if you would like to learn more about these terms.

The term suffering is used in many mental health texts. However, its use on a continuum to help distinguish the mental health client, who is suffering, from the coachable client, who is surviving, comes from Dr. Rosenbaum's teachings. His training and reference series, *Beat Depression & Anxiety Now!*, covers this topic.

## Contemplation Letter # 3

Again, the use of the term surviving to describe a client who is appropriate for Life Coaching services comes from Dr. Rosenbaum's training at ASPLC.

The word collaborate is a hallmark Life Coaching word. It is found in Life Coaching text after Life Coaching text. I first heard it in relationship to coaching from Dr. Rosenbaum. I first encountered it in print form in Dr. Patrick Williams' and Dr. Diane Menendez's book, *Becoming a Professional Life Coach: Lessons from the Institute of Life Coach Training, 2nd Edition.*

Thinking SpaceTM is the phrase I selected to describe the space shared by the Life Coach and client where the coaching conversation occurs. I like the term for its simplicity. Its formal definition includes concepts developed by Dr. Rosenbaum. Thus, it is a shared trademark.

The term challenge, used instead of the term confront, is one I first encountered during my psychology training. I can name neither the exact professor who discussed it nor the book in which I first saw it printed. However, it was part of my training at FIT. It is and has always been my preferred term for professionally contradicting a client in a manner meant to help the client move forward and grow. Dr. Patrick Williams and Dr. Diane Menendez include in their text, *Becoming a Professional Life Coach: Lessons from the Institute of Life Coach Training, 2nd Edition*, a term called compassionate edge, which is a good term that includes a helpful description for the importance of challenging a client while maintaining empathy.

The term block comes from CBT. It has several variations. My favorite is stumbling block as I believe it helps create for the client the idea that the block is temporary, a hang up, not a permanent impediment.

## Contemplation Letter # 4

My awareness of the different varieties and specialties in coaching comes from many sources, too many to remember and name. However, I will say that Tony Stoltzfus's book, *Coaching Questions: A Coach's Guide to Powerful Asking Skills*, lists a few of the more common specialties in coaching and provides a brief overview of their specialized skill sets. A quick search on the internet is another good way to acquaint yourself with the professional focuses available in the coaching field.

## Contemplation Letter # 5

Ethics are an essential part of any formal career path. In fact, the development of ethics and best practices is often what marks a career track as officially a career track. Its what makes both other professionals and the public take the profession seriously. A great starting point for further research into Life Coaching ethics is *Law and Ethics in Coaching: How to Solve – and Avoid – Difficult Problems in Your Practice* by Dr. Patrick Williams and Dr. Sharon K. Anderson.

My familiarity with the availability of degrees and coaching comes from several sources. First, I chose the school I attended based on research into different certificates and degrees. Second, as part of my introduction to coaching during my training at ASPLC, I was introduced to more information on coaching that included the basic educational pathways through specialty certifications. Also, Dr. Patrick Williams and Dr. Diane Menendez cover coach training options in *Becoming a Professional Life Coach: Lessons from the Institute of Life Coach Training, 2nd Edition*. In order to make sure you are getting the most up-to-date information, I would suggest you do some internet research on available programs. One good place to start is the International Coach Federation (ICF) website: www.coachfederation.org. The ICF's website lists schools that meet their standards of education.

Transformation is a word that is found in many places. My first exposure to it in regard to Life Coaching comes from *The 5 Levels of Listening: Becoming a Transformation Listener* by Dr. Elliott B. Rosenbaum.

## Contemplation Letter # 6

Information about the International Coach Federation (ICF), its purpose, and its available credentialing can be found at: www.coachfederation.org. The information included in this book is the most up-to-date information that was available at the time of the book's writing. Since organizations and the products and services they offer can always change, I recommend that you visit the ICF's website to address any questions you may have as well as to double check the most recent requirements of any of their certifications.

Information about the International Association of Coaching (IAC), its purpose, and its available credentialing can be found at: certifiedcoach.org. The information included in this book is the most up-to-date information that was available at the time of the book's writing. Since organizations and the products and services they offer can always change, I recommend that you visit the IAC's website to address any questions you may have as well as to double check the most recent requirements of any of their certifications.

## Determination Letter # 1

The concept of metas can be found in many different branches of learning: philosophy, psychology, communication, etc. I am not able to recall when I first encountered the prefix, meta, though I would estimate it was during my undergraduate education as part of a class. Since then, I have encountered numerous versions of the use of meta-. Metacommunication and metathinking are a large part of coaching and can be found in many coaching texts.

The definition of wisdom as a combination of the information provided by thinking and feeling comes from Dr. Marsha M. Linehan's work with Dialectical Behavior Therapy (DBT). She posits that the wise mind comes from the rational mind and the emotional mind. Her original text is *Cognitive-Behavioral Treatment of Borderline Personality Disorder*. A great basic explanation of the wise mind can also be found in *Don't Let Your Emotions Run Your Life for Teens: Dialectical Behavior Therapy Skills for Helping You Manage Mood Swings, Control Angry Outbursts, and Get Along with Others* by Sheri Ven Dijk, M.S.W.

## Determination Letter # 2

The idea of support is, again, a common one. The distinction that Life Coaching is primarily a means of support for the client is a fundamental part of any significant Life Coaching text. Thus, there is not single person I can credit this concept to though perhaps the best person to cite here is Thomas J. Leonard, who is considered the founding father of personal coaching. He established several coach training institutions, including Coach U and Coachville, as well as created the two most prominent coaching organizations to date, the ICF and the IAC. One of his most popular books is *The Portable Coach: 28 Surefire Strategies for Business and Personal Success*. In addition, in the realm of support, a nice compendium of supportive Life Coaching techniques can be found in *Total Life Coaching: 50+ Life Lessons, Skills, and Techniques to Enhance Your Practice...and Your Life* by Dr. Patrick Williams and Dr. Lloyd J. Thomas.

## Determination Letter # 3

Celebration is a concept that is core to Life Coaching. Clients are encouraged to recognize both their efforts and outcomes and to celebrate both. I first encountered the importance of celebration in Life Coaching through my training with Dr. Rosenbaum.

## Action Letter # 1

The idea of roles and role conflict is a concept I first encountered during a women's studies course at the University of Central Florida (UCF). The primary textbook for the class was *Women: Images and Reality, A Multicultural Anthology* by Dr. Suzanne Kelly, Dr. Gowri Parameswaran, and Dr. Nancy Schniedewind, which is now available in its fifth edition.

## Action Letter # 2

The mentioned modes of learning, cited here in concept though not by official names, come from Neil Fleming's VARK Model of learning that designates that learners often have a preferred mode of learning, which is either visual, auditory, reading/writing, or kinesthetic. Further information about these learning styles can be found in *Teaching and Learning Styles: VARK Strategies* by Neil Fleming.

## Action Letter # 3

The reference to balking and quaking and gritting your teeth are loose references to the stages of adjustment I often use in my clinical work as a psychologist, which are based on the grieving stages observed and described formally by Dr. Elisabeth Kübler-Ross. According to her research, there are five stages of grief: Denial, Anger, Bargaining, Depression, and Acceptance, which can be thought of as DABDA, for short. I replace the word Acceptance with Acknowledgement to describe the fifth stage due to the connotations of the word acceptance. Often, people see acceptance as saying something is okay. Some life events are not ones that a person will ever say are okay. True processing of a significant event requires not saying it is okay but acknowledging that it happened so thoughts, feelings, and decisions are based in reality not the fantasy that it never occurred or can be made to unhappen. Further reading can by done on the stages of grief in *On Grief and Grieving: Finding the Meaning of Grief Through the Five Stages of Loss* by Dr. Elisabeth Kübler-Ross and David Kessler.

## Action Letter # 4

This further expansion of the prefix meta and its relationship to important words in coaching, including metacommunication, metabehavior, metathinking, and metafeeling, is again attributable to many different branches of learning, including philosophy, psychology, communication, etc. More information can be found in a wide array of Life Coaching texts.

The importance of metaphor in coaching was first introduced to me by Dr. Patrick Williams during a training class as part of my curriculum at ASPLC. During the class, he covered the prominence of metaphor in conversation, including the coaching conversation, as well as the importance of using clean language. One of the preeminent books on metaphor is *Metaphors We Live By* by Dr. George Lakoff and Dr. Mark Johnson. Related to the use of metaphor in coaching is the concept of clean language. David Grove created the clean language approach in the 1980s. *The Work and Life of David Grove: Clean Language and Emergent Knowledge*, a comprehensive book about his life and accomplishments, was written by Carol Wilson.

The distinction between doing and being a coach is covered across many books and texts. I first encountered the distinction during training at ASPLC with Dr. Rosenbaum. A book that spends some time working through the distinction is Dr. Patrick Williams' and Dr. Diane

Menendez's text, *Becoming a Professional Life Coach: Lessons from the Institute of Life Coach Training, 2nd Edition*.

Reframing is a hallmark of Cognitive-Behavioral Therapy. It was during by study of psychology at FIT that I first came across the term. I most often encounter it in CBT texts. Dr. Judith Beck's book, *Cognitive Behavior Therapy: Basics and Beyond, Second Edition*, is a good place to start if you would like to learn more about reframing and see it in use.

## Action Letter # 5

The S.M.A.R.T Goal Method, also known as SMART Goals, was first written about by George T. Doran in the 1980s. The approach was initially developed to help managers with their day-to-day oversight and guidance of employees. Since then, SMART Goals have been incorporated into many different fields, including psychology and coaching. I first encountered the S.M.A.R.T. Goal Method in a graduate course at FIT.

## Action Letter # 6

The concept of an ideal client is, again, found in many different Life Coaching texts and on many different Life Coaching websites. I first encountered the idea of an ideal client in psychology training. I first encountered the idea of an ideal Life Coaching client during my training at ASPLC. A good discussion of the importance of identifying and working with ideal clients can be found in Michael Port's *Book Yourself Solid: The Fastest, Easiest, and Most Reliable System for Getting More Clients Than You Can Handle Even if You Hate Marketing and Selling, Third Edition*.

The term welcome packet is one that is used more in Life Coaching than psychology. I first encountered the term during my training at ASPLC. A good place to start in developing your own welcome packet is to review the forms found in Dr. Patrick Williams' and Dr. Deborah C. Davis' book, *Therapist as Life Coach: An Introduction for Counselors and Other Helping Professionals, Revised and Expanded*. The ICF also has forms on its website: www.coachfederation.org.

## Action Letter # 7

The concept of flow is one I first encountered during my study of psychology. The original text on flow is *Flow: The Psychology of Optimal Experience* by Dr. Mihaly Csikszentmihalyi.

## Action Letter # 8

The Life Wheel, also known as the Coaching Mandala or Wheel of Life, can be found in many different Life Coaching texts. Many versions are available online. The version I first saw in print can be found in Dr. Patrick Williams' and Dr. Diane Menendez's book, *Becoming a Professional Life Coach: Lessons from the Institute of Life Coach Training, 2nd Edition*.

## Renewal Letter

Self-actualization is a term coined by Dr. Abraham H. Maslow. It is the final stage of his original version of the Hierarchy of Needs. A later version, which is not as popular and, thus, not often cited in either psychology or coaching literature, lists Transcendence as the highest stage.

I first encountered the term coachability in Tony Stoltzfus's book, *Coaching Questions: A Coach's Guide to Powerful Asking Skills*. The concept, which goes by several different names, can be found in many Life Coaching texts.

The difference between being childlike and childish was a distinction I first encountered in the coaching world during a training with Dr. Patrick Williams.

The concept of powerful questions, also known as thought-provoking questions is found across Life Coaching literature. I first encountered the concept of powerful questions during my training with Dr. Rosenbaum at ASPLC. A great resource for coaches who are just starting out and want to increase their repertoire of powerful asking questions is Tony Stoltzfus's book, *Coaching Questions: A Coach's Guide to Powerful Asking Skills*.

Clean language is a term and method created by David Grove in the 1980s. *The Work and Life of David Grove: Clean Language and*

*Emergent Knowledge*, a comprehensive book about his life and accomplishments, was written by Carol Wilson. It is a good place to start if you would like to know more about clean language or its creator.

Mindfulness is a concept that originated with Eastern philosophies of health and wellness. Often cited in texts about Buddhism, mindfulness has made its way into the psychology and Life Coaching literature. A mindfulness workbook that I have found to be helpful for people is *A Mindfulness-Based Stress Reduction Workbook* by Dr. Bob Stahl and Dr. Elisha Goldstein.

Shoulds are a form of a thinking error that is covered in Dr. Judith Beck's book, *Cognitive Behavior Therapy: Basics and Beyond, Second Edition*. For more information on shoulds and other thinking errors, Dr. Beck's book is a great place to start.

## Maintenance Letter

The emotion words listed here, confusion, frustration, happiness, sadness, and worry, are based on the five feeling system I use in my therapy work as it is simple and easily accessible by client. There are many different versions of feeling categories found in psychology. Again, the interactions between thoughts, feelings, and behaviors come from the Cognitive Behavioral Therapy model.

The concept of searching your life for other forms of success so you can replicate them comes from Positive Psychology and Solutions-Oriented Brief Therapy. A great text on the use of solutions-oriented questions is *Interviewing for Solutions, Fourth Edition* by Dr. Peter De Jong and Insoo Kim Berg.

## Legacy Letter

The concept of legacy is based on Erik Erikson's psychosocial stage, Generativity vs, Stagnation, and can be found in his Theory of Psychosocial Development.

Gratitude has been found to be a significant contributor to happiness. It relates to a concept called satisfaction with abilities, which I first studied as part of my graduate thesis, *The Relationship between*

*Functional Impairment, Satisfaction with Ability, and Psychological Well-Being in Older Adults with Arthritis*, for which Dr. Thomas H. Harrell was my chair. The relationship between satisfaction with abilities and gratitude is that recognizing and appreciating what you have leads to more happiness. Those people who are satisfied, or grateful, for what they have or what they can do fare better mentally and emotionally than those who are not satisfied, or are not grateful; this is true regardless of the actual abilities a person has or the life challenges they are facing. There are many books, articles, and websites on happiness. Two recent popular books on happiness are *The Book of Joy: Lasting Happiness in a Changing World* by His Holiness the Dalai Lama and Archbishop Desmond Tutu and *The Blue Zones of Happiness: Lessons from the World's Happiest People* by Dan Buettner.

## Closing Letter

The word request is a word that is common in Life Coaching. It underscores the concept that the Life Coach and the client are equals. Thus, orders are not given. I first encountered the concept of making a request of clients during my graduate psychology training. My most thorough education in the art of making requests of clients occurred during my internship and post-doctoral years. My first experience with making requests of coaching clients came during my training at ASPLC.

# THE POST SCRIPTS

## Common Concepts

The definitions in the Common Concepts section for each word were created by me. The descriptions for the Life Coach's role and the client's role found in the Further Thoughts section are also my descriptions.

The majority of the terminology I incorporated into this section results from my reading of the following books, which I have listed in alphabetical order by title:

*Becoming a Professional Life Coach: Lessons from the Institute of Life Coach Training, 2nd Edition* by Dr. Patrick Williams and Dr. Diane S Menendez

*Book Yourself Solid: The Fastest, Easiest, and Most Reliable System for Getting More Clients Than You Can Handle Even if You Hate Marketing and Selling, Third Edition* by Michael Port

*Coaching Questions: A Coach's Guide to Powerful Asking Skills* by Tony Stoltzfus

*The Essential Self: The Key to a Life of Passion, Lasting Joy, and Fulfillment* by Dr. Elliott B. Rosenbaum

*Flow: The Psychology of Optimal Experience* by Dr. Mihaly Csikszentmihalyi

*Law and Ethics in Coaching: How to Solve – and Avoid – Difficult Problems in Your Practice* by Dr. Patrick Williams and Dr. Sharon K. Anderson

*Strengths Finder 2.0* by Tom Rath

*Therapist as Life Coach: An Introduction for Counselors and Other Helping Professionals, Revised and Expanded* by Dr. Patrick Williams and Dr. Deborah C. Davis

*Time to Think: Listening to Ignite the Human Mind* by Nancy Kline

*Total Life Coaching: 50+ Life Lessons, Skills, and Techniques to Enhance Your Practice...and Your Life* by Dr. Patrick Williams and Dr. Lloyd J. Thomas

*The Valued Self: Five Steps to Healthy Self-Esteem* by Dr. Elliott B. Rosenbaum

*

The designation of Life Coaching as having four primary elements, which I refer to as the four pillars of Life Coaching, comes from my training at the American School of Professional Life Coaching, directed by Dr. Elliott B Rosenbaum. This descriptor for Life Coaching's basic tenets can be found in many of the term's definitions.

# AFTER THE WORDS

Dear Young Life Coach,

It is my sincere hope that this book has been helpful to you in some way. I have sought to create an atmosphere of gentleness and hoped to infuse at least a sentence or two with grace. If even a hint of my intention has come through, I consider this book a success and myself blessed.

As for you, Young Life Coach, no matter where you are in your coaching journey or your life journey, I wish you the best. The health and beauty of the world is dependent upon the health and beauty of the individuals in it.

So, be strong. Be bold. Be gentle. Be understanding. Be compassionate. Be wise.

Be You.

Each and every breathtaking facet of you. The world needs you. It wants you. And I for one feel fortunate to have shared space—the pages of this book—with you.

It's been a pleasure to meet you, Young Life Coach. I look forward to all that you choose to do.

Sincerely,
Faith

# APPRECIATIONS

Thanks go to Dr. Elliott B. Rosenbaum for his mentorship and guidance. His patience, warmth, and professionalism are evident in everything he does. And his books are important additions to the fields of Life Coaching and psychology. This project would not exist without him.

Thanks to Dr. Patrick Williams for being one of the original pioneers of Life Coaching. The strides he has made in helping define the field for the public as well as in educating those interested in joining its ranks cannot be underestimated. His books provide a foundation for Life Coaches as well as a point of aspiration. Life Coaching owes him a great debt. And I greatly enjoyed learning from him.

Thanks also go to the many Young Life Coaches I have met along the way. Their willingness to share their experiences, their openness to inviting me into the fold, and their bravery in taking one more life step are much admired. Thank you all.

## ABOUT THE CORRESPONDENT

Dr. Faith Powers is a Licensed Psychologist, Master Certified Life Coach, and consultant. She received her Doctorate of Psychology (Psy.D.) from the Florida Institute of Technology (FIT) and her Certified Life Coach and Master Certified Life Coach certificates from the American School of Professional Life Coaching.

*Letters to a Young Life Coach* is her first publication in the field of Life Coaching. She can be reached via her business website: www.thinkwellcoachingandconsulting.com.

# INDEX